CUSTOMIZED VERSION OF

ANYBODY'S GUIDE TO TOTAL FITNESS

LEN KRAVITZ

DESIGNED SPECIFICALLY FOR
LANSING COMMUNITY
COLLEGE

D0084167

Kendall Hunt
publishing company

Kendall Hunt
publishing company

www.kendallhunt.com
Send all inquiries to:
4050 Westmark Drive
Dubuque, IA 52004-1840

Dedicated with love to my mom,
who always believed in me

CONTENTS

PREFACE

Anybody's Guide to Total Fitness tenth edition combines the most up-to-date scientific and practical information for establishing an optimal health, fitness and wellness lifestyle. The tenth edition incorporates the American College of Sport's Medicine's latest guidelines for health, weight management and physical activity. The text offers instruction on how to customize exercise programs for mixed impact aerobics, indoor cycling, step training, aerobic kickboxing, circuit training, functional exercise, boot camp programs, interval training and aquatic workouts. Specific advice on yoga, Pilates and mind-body fitness is also provided.

Readers will learn about several contemporary health issues including self-concept, substance abuse, responsible drinking, tobacco use, stress maintenance, technostress, creative problem solving and time management. The tenth edition simplifies modern-day research on cortisol and body weight, high-protein and low-carbohydrate diets, fat burner supplements and energy balance. Sound nutritional concepts for a healthy existence are discussed.

What elevates this text are the over 200 biomechanically correct fitness illustrations by Jill Pankey. A full compliment of flexibility, strength, core, stability ball and targeted exercises are presented and explained. In addition, the tenth edition provides credible and insightful answers to 125 frequently asked questions about fitness. Included are all-inclusive sections dispelling numerous exercise myths and correcting common mistakes in health and fitness.

The profile guide that accompanies the text is a behavioral modification planner and assessment supplement that promotes positive, self-directed goal attainment. Both inspirationally and practically, *Anybody's Guide to Total Fitness* tenth edition is a wonderful source for long-term health and fitness success.

ACKNOWLEDGMENTS

I would like to express my deep appreciation and gratitude to my original editorial advisory board of Dr. Carol L. Christensen, Dr. Craig J. Cisar, Dr. Gail G. Evans, Dr. Susan Kutner, Lori Leeds, R.P.T., Dr. Thomas A. MacLean, Dr. Susan Pate, Dr. Robert Pearl, Dr. Jay D. Pruzansky, Dr. Norman T. Reynolds, Richard V. Schroeder, M.S., and Dr. Phillip A. Sienna. Their advice, expertise, and thoughtful review of this book were invaluable.

I sincerely thank the following people who have made generous contributions to this project and deserve special acknowledgment: Emmanuel Athans, Molly Burke, Mert and Tanya Carpenter, Kim Drummond, Janice Earle, Carrie Ekins, Eric Finch, Dixie Fisher, Sue Forster-Cox, Glenda Gilliam, Marla Graves, Jerry Gonsalves, Jean Harding, Louise Herndon, Michael Le Doux, Shirley H. M. Reekie, Pauline Reimer, Joe Samuels, Wendy Russum, Dolores Sargent, Amy Scofield, Carol Stewart, Ph.D., Debbie Sporleder, Carol Sullivan, Pamela Staver, and Teri Wexted.

I would also like to thank the following special people who have been a source of inspiration and have guided me in countless ways: Covert Bailey, Dr. Barton Byers, Dr. Laurence Berkowitz, Ed and Shirley Burke, Don Callahan, Roy Cerrito, Retta Chavkin, Dr. Barbara Conry, Yvonne Cotton, Peter and Kathie Davis, Justine Dineen, Anita Del Grande, Jerry Dollard, Dr. Jacqueline Douglass, Ronda Gates, Dr. Telemachos A. Greanias, Dr. William F. Gustafson, C. Lansing Hays, Ellen Herbst, Dr. Vivian H. Heyward, Dr. Clair W. Jennett, DeAun Kizer, Bob Kravitz, Joyce Malone, Frank Napier, Dr. Bruce Ogilvie, Lawrence R. Petulla, Doug Sporleder, Marty Urand, and Neil Wiley.

For their enthusiastic support, I am grateful to my friends at the Los Gatos Athletic Club, the faculty and staff of the Department of Kinesiology at San Jose State University, and everyone at Aerobics Plus.

I am also deeply indebted to my friend Chuck Drummond for providing such wise counsel and friendship.

To Dr. Susan Pate, my original editor and lifetime friend, I thank you in a thousand different ways.

To Jill Pankey, my illustrator, I thank you for your artistic imagination and for the many hours of hard work you devoted to this book to make it come to life.

ABOUT THE AUTHOR

Len Kravitz, Ph.D., is the program coordinator of Exercise Science and researcher at the University of New Mexico where he won the "Outstanding Teacher of the Year" award (2004). Len was honored with the 1999 Canadian Fitness Professional "International Presenter of the Year", the 2006 Canadian Fitness Professional "Specialty Presenter of the Year" award, the American Council on Exercise 2006 "Fitness Educator of the Year", and the 2010 Global Award for his contributions to the Aquatic Exercise Association. Len has authored more than 180 articles on health and fitness for several national publications and has been featured on *CNN News, Dateline* and CBS *This Morning.*

Dr. Kravitz is a versatile movement specialist with a broad range of skills, which include competitive gymnastics at the national and international levels and professional theater/mime performances on stage and video. He is the creator of *Anybody's Workout, Anybody's 3-in-1 Workout, Anybody's Step Workout,* and the *SuperAbs* exercise videos, which have been featured in national magazines and TV shows. Len's innovative technique and teaching style have made him a sought-after lecturer for fitness professionals around the United States, Canada, Australia, Europe, Taiwan, and Japan.

WELCOME TO A HEALTHY WAY OF LIFE

Living and enjoying life to its fullest is a wonderful goal. And you can have it! Fitness is a way of life that allows you to function and perform at your best. It's a harmonic balance of prescribed exercise, healthy eating habits, preventative health care, effective stress management, and a common-sense lifestyle. Your level of fitness helps determine the quality of your life. You are in control of how you look, feel, and live.

The following information is based on sound physiological principles and research. With a minimal investment of your time, you can follow these concepts and create a fitness plan that will help you obtain the most from your life.

I have presented a specific aerobics program for you. You may wish to supplement it with a running, swimming, or cycling program of your own.

Be patient, use your knowledge, set your goals, listen to your body, and commit yourself to a healthy way of life.

KEYS TO SUCCESS
FOR ALL LCC FITNESS CENTER CLASSES

▶ *ALL* STUDENTS MUST COMPLETE AN ORIENTATION during the first week of the semester. This includes students new to the Fitness Center and all returning students. Orientation instructions are on Desire to Learn (D2L) on the LCC website, or at either LCC Fitness Center.

▶ ATTENDANCE VERIFICATION (COLLEGE POLICY): or you will be dropped from the class.

▶ STUDENTS ARE RESPONSIBLE FOR CHECKING D2L AND THEIR LCC EMAIL REGULARLY—DAILY IS RECOMMENDED!
  ☐ Course information, including assignments, schedules, and other information is on the Desire to Learn (D2L) course management system.

  ☐ Information and reminders will be sent via LCC email.

  ☐ If you do not receive emails, or if you are unable to access the internet for any reason, students are still responsible for all assignments, information, and deadlines.

▶ IF YOU DO NOT KNOW HOW TO ACCESS ANGEL OR LCC EMAIL, GO TO AN LCC COMPUTER CENTER FOR ASSISTANCE!

  ☐ Students are responsible for completing the course requirements regardless of their ability to access D2L or LCC email.

▶ GRADES ARE KEPT IN YOUR FOLDER IN THE FITNESS CENTER. ASK ANY INSTRUCTOR TO REVIEW YOUR FOLDER AND CHECK YOUR GRADE.

  ☐ Grades and attendance information will not be given out by phone or email. You must come in to either Fitness Center to check your grade.

▶ ATTEND THE FITNESS CENTER AND COMPLETE YOUR WORKOUTS EARLY IN THE SEMESTER! Work out on a regular basis starting at the beginning of the semester.

▶ QUESTIONS? Ask any Instructor at either Fitness Center!

The Fitness Center Faculty wants YOU to earn a good grade in your Fitness Center Class!

LCC Fitness Center Policies

► **ATTENDANCE and PARTICIPATION**

  ☐ **Student MUST bring their StarCard to enter the Fitness Center.**

  ☐ Only students who are enrolled in Fitness Center Classes may work out in the Fitness Center.

► **PERSONAL PROPERTY**

  ☐ Personal items (back packs, coats, gym bags, and other items) may NOT be brought into the Fitness Center. Personal items must be locked in a locker or left in the student's car.

  ☐ The PFW Department is not responsible for lost, stolen, or misplaced property.

► **WORKOUT CLOTHING**

  ☐ Appropriate gym attire must be worn when working out in either Fitness Center. Be sure workout gear is not overly revealing when bending, stretching, and moving. Gym clothes must be clean and odor free.

  ☐ **ACCEPTABLE:** T-shirt (shirt required), shorts, sweats, warm-ups, athletic shoes.

  ☐ **NOT ALLOWED:** Street clothes (including jeans or jean shorts), cargo pants or cargo shorts, street shoes, sandals, crocs.

► **CELL PHONE POLICY**

  ☐ Personal electronic devices (including cell phones) may be used for listening to music ONLY! Talking, texting, internet, or other uses are prohibited.

  ☐ Use of cameras or cell phone cameras in the fitness center, locker rooms, pool, and weight room are prohibited.

► **INSURANCE**   It is recommended that each student have a health and accident insurance policy. Information regarding insurance can be obtained at the Student and Academic Support Divisional Office located in room 211 of the Student Personal Services Building. It should be noted that each student is responsible for providing his/her own coverage.

► **HEALTH WAIVER**   An annual physical examination is strongly recommended. Each student must file a completed health information sheet and waiver with his/her instructor.

► **CONCERNS**   Please direct all concerns to: Department Chair, Physical Fitness & Wellness, Room 351, Gannon Building, or call 483-1227.

LOCKS AND LOCKERS POLICIES

▶ **LOCKS and LOCKERS**

☐ **MAIN CAMPUS**

- Students may bring their own lock and lock their personal items in any open locker in the locker room while they are working out. Personal locks may not be left on lockers overnight.

- Lockers can be rented for the semester in Room 281 GB (Control Center) for $2 per semester with a $2 lock deposit. The $2 lock deposit will be returned if the lock is returned on or before the last day of class.

- Long lockers may be used only during student's activity class. Locks left on long lockers outside of class time may have their locks removed and articles confiscated.

☐ **WEST CAMPUS**

- Lockers are available on a DAILY BASIS WHILE ATTENDING YOUR ACTIVITY CLASS.

- Students may check out a lock for the duration of the activity class at the fitness center desk at no charge. Return your lock to the desk when finished with your workout. Personal locks left on a locker will be cut off ½ hour after the fitness center closes. Locker contents will be confiscated.

▶ **DELINQUENT LOCKER OCCUPATION**

☐ Articles left in a locker following the posted deadline for the semester may be removed and discarded.

▶ **TOWELS**

☐ Towels are included in activity class lab fee. Lost towel fee is $4 per towel.

▶ **MAIN CAMPUS** Students may sign out a towel for the entire semester at the Control Center. The student must exchange a dirty towel for a clean towel. *AT THE END OF THE SEMESTER, THE STUDENT IS RESPONSIBLE TO MAKE CERTAIN THAT HIS/HER NAME IS CROSSED OFF THE CLASS TOWEL LIST IN RED UPON RETURNING THE TOWEL.* Holds may be placed on the student record if the towel is not returned by the posted deadline.

▶ **WEST CAMPUS** Students may sign out a towel at the beginning of class each day and must return the towel at the end of each class.

SET S-M-A-R-T GOALS!

Setting goals is an important part of your Fitness Plan. If you don't have goals, how will you know if you have accomplished what you set out to accomplish? Goals help us measure our progress, stay motivated, and continue to improve.

Think about what you want to accomplish and how you plan to get there. Your goals should be S-M-A-R-T!

S- Specific: Goals such as "Lose weight," or "Get stronger," are not specific. Goals such as "Lose 10 pounds by the end of the semester," or "Be able to lift 100 pounds on the chest press by May 1," are specific goals.

M- Measurable: A goal of "Get in shape" or "Tone up" are not easily measured. A goal of "Be able to jog for 30 minutes without stopping" can be measured and when you do it, you know it! Measurable goals must include a specific number or amount, such as time, distance, weight, number of repetitions, frequency, etc.

A- Achievable: A goal of "I want to lift 500 pounds on the bench press," may not be achievable. A goal of "To weigh 118 pounds," may not be achievable if your height and body type are not compatible with that weight. Make your goals large enough to be challenging, yet small enough to be reached within a reasonable time period so you can then take the next step.

R- Relevant: Choose goals that are relevant to YOU! You are more likely to be motivated to reach goals that align with your interests and abilities. A goal of, "I will do a swim workout three mornings per week," is probably not very realistic if you are not a good swimmer and you hate getting up early! If you like to dance, a more relevant goal might be, "I will dance along with a 30 minute dance exercise video three times per week for 10 weeks." Make your goal something you want to do!

T- Timely: This refers to both your time schedule and the time available to reach the goal. If your schedule is already full, and you set a goal to work out for two hours every day, chances are that you will not be able to meet that goal. Similarly, if you decide on May 1 that you want to lose 30 pounds before your friend's wedding on May 15, you have little chance of success. A long term goal needs a long term time commitment, with smaller goals leading up to it.

If you need help developing your daily intermediate or long term goals, talk with any instructor! Your instructor can help you evaluate your goals and measure your progress. After a goal has been reached, set new goals. If your goals have not been met, re-evaluate both your goals and strategies to see how you can get on track to meet those goals.

EXERCISE + ACADEMICS = SUCCESS

Everyone knows that participating in physical activity will help to improve your fitness level, help you to maintain a desirable weight, and lower your risk of many chronic diseases such as heart disease, type 2 diabetes, osteoporosis, and some cancers. However, there is a lot of exciting research relating higher fitness levels with improved academic scores! Across the country, there are research articles, news interviews, and books informing people about the relationship between physical activity and learning.

Research shows that the fitness of your body is related to the fitness of your brain. This means that the more fit you are, the more likely you are to score well on tests and have better grades! Many scientists are saying that exercise is like "Miracle Grow" for the brain. Exercise activates the release of "BDNF" which is a neuron growth factor that improves cognition by growing new brain cells, stimulates our brain to keep us alert, lowers stress, improves memory, and puts the brain in the optimal learning environment.

In 2001, The California Department of Education and University of Illinois discovered fit students performed 2 times better on academic tests compared to their unfit peers. The University of Illinois discovered that students who were fit demonstrated better attention; which reduced their mistakes when taking tests. The fit students were able to use "executive function," which is the way students are able to process information. Improved executive function allows students to slow down, evaluate correct choices, and make changes in areas they have previously made mistakes.

The Centers of Disease Control and Prevention (CDC, 2010) released a report summarizing the relationship between physical activity and academic achievement. This report led to formal recommendations encouraging schools to incorporate physical activity into their curriculum. Exercise has been shown to improve standardized test scores, grade point average (GPA), attention, and even behavioral issues.

Exercise feeds the brain glucose (energy) and oxygen which helps to build better connections between neurons (brain cells). These neurons help the brain to read, write, and compute. Scientists have discovered that exercise has the most effect on the Hippocampus, which is the portion of the brain that helps short term memory convert into long term memory. Physically active students have more neuron connections than inactive classmates. The increase in Hippocampus activity allows active students to focus better and improve their memory.

Tips to get the most brain power from your workout:

▶ Regularly participate in an exercise program 3 to 5 times per week. Incorporate aerobic exercises that you enjoy!

▶ Engage in moderate intensity aerobic exercise for 20–60 minutes 1–2 hours before a difficult class, especially if you have a test.

▶ If you don't have time to exercise before class, perform any type of exercise that increases your heart rate and breathing rate such as: briskly walking across campus, taking the stairs instead of the elevator, or parking further away from campus.

▶ Engage in an Activity Break at *www.lcc.edu* "Activity Breaks." These are designed to stimulate the learning centers of the brain. Once these centers are activated, you will have more energy and be able to focus your attention on your studies.

▶ Engage Brain Break exercises at *www.lcc.edu* "Brain Breaks." These are quick 1 to 2 minute activities that engage both sides of the brain. These activities are designed to improve your attention and increase your ability to focus, which are important components of learning!

It's not a coincidence that the Physical Fitness & Wellness (PFW) Department's slogan is "Fit Body—Fit Mind." We are thrilled with this slogan because for years we have known that a fit body makes for a fit mind. However, now there is an abundant amount of research to back it up! What are you waiting for? Get up, get moving, and start learning!

Section 1
Starting Out

What Exercise Will Do for You

Benefits of a well-balanced health and fitness program are:

- A healthy appearance
- Good posture and alignment
- Fluid, easy movement
- Stronger joints and firmer muscles
- Lowered risk for low-back pain
- A decreased susceptibility to injury
- Fewer aches and pains
- A more efficient circulatory and respiratory system
- Lowered risk of cardiovascular disease and stroke
- Improved blood cholesterol levels
- Better control of blood pressure
- Increased life expectancy
- A decrease in body fat and/or body weight
- Controlled appetite
- Better digestion
- Improved mental awareness, self-esteem, and self-confidence
- Improved ability to relax
- Better handling of stress
- Help in preventing and coping with depression
- More restful sleep
- Increased job productivity
- More energy and vitality
- AN INCREASED ABILITY TO ENJOY LIFE

Stickin' to It!

Tips for Exercise Success

These tips will steer you toward success in exercise.

1. **Write out a health and fitness evaluation list**—what you do right (don't smoke, good eating habits, no substance abuse, etc.) and what you need to correct (lack of regular exercise, poor posture, high emotional stress, etc.). Next, figure out what you can do to shift more entries to the "right" side.

2. **Set realistic long- and short-term goals.** Make sure you break them down into manageable steps. Write this out like a personal contract, including objectives of your health and fitness action plan and the date you plan to start specific activities. Solicit the support of someone close to you. Keep track of your progress, revising your fitness plan if needed, and reward yourself as goals are achieved (a show, a new outfit, a book, etc.).

3. **Find a workout companion** with a fitness level and goals similar to yours. Pick some exercise activities or classes that you both enjoy, and commit to participating in them. Talk to other individuals who have reached goals similar to yours. Find out what strategies helped them keep on track.

> **Did You Know?**
>
> More than half of the people who start an exercise program drop out after six months.

4. **Schedule your exercise three to five days per week.** Choose a "special" time of day, and be selfish about preserving that time for your body and general well-being.

5. **Listen to your body and progress slowly in the beginning.** Most injuries in fitness come from doing too much, too soon, too fast, and too hard.

6. **Don't let early awkwardness or uneven skill development get you down.** It happens to everyone. And try not to compare yourself to others.

7. **Wear comfortable exercise clothing and proper shoes.** Your clothing should permit you to move freely and allow your body to cool itself. Do not wear fabrics that hinder evaporation.

8. **Plan your exercise** at least two hours after or at least an hour before a big meal.

9. **Be patient;** exercise has many immediate and delayed benefits. Your time will come! Don't get angry at yourself if you miss a workout or slip on a health goal. Try to focus on what caused the lapse and how you may better deal with it in the future. Most importantly, stay positive and believe in yourself. You are in control.

10. **Be aware of the signs of overexertion:** breathlessness, dizziness, tightness or pain in the chest, loss of muscle control, and nausea. If you experience any of these signs, stop immediately. See your physician to determine the cause. Also, don't exercise if you are sick.

Five Key Components of Fitness

Your body is a complex organism designed for action. Being physically fit means that the heart, blood vessels, lungs, and muscles function at optimal efficiency. Following are five key components of health-related physical fitness with which you need to be concerned.

Did You Know?

By giving up smoking, doing regular exercise and cutting excess weight you can elevate your HDL (good) cholesterol.

1. **Cardiorespiratory Endurance/Aerobic Conditioning** is the ability of the body's heart, lungs, blood vessels, and major muscle groups to persist in continuous rhythmic exercise such as brisk walking, jogging, swimming, aerobics, rowing, cycling, step training, skating, and cross-country skiing. Regular aerobic conditioning may prevent or reduce the likelihood of cardiovascular disease. Cardiorespiratory endurance is the most important component of health-related fitness.

2. **Muscular Strength** is the ability of the muscles to exert maximal or near maximal force against resistance. Stronger muscles protect the joints that they surround and reduce the incidence of injury from physical activity.

   An increase in muscle mass will also boost the body's metabolism.

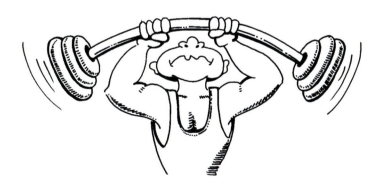

3. **Muscular Endurance** is the ability of skeletal muscle to exert force (not necessarily maximal) over an extended period of time. Strength, skill, performance, speed of movement, and power are closely associated with this component. Muscular endurance helps to prevent injuries and improve posture.

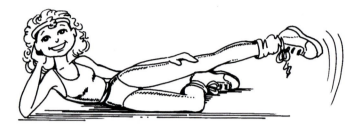

4. **Flexibility** is the range of motion of the muscles and joints of the body. It has to do with your skeletal muscles' natural and conditioned ability to extend beyond their normal resting length. Increased flexibility will enhance performance and reduce the incidence of injury.

5. **Body Composition** is the relationship of percentage of body fat to lean body weight (muscle, bone, water, vital organs). Being overfat, which usually starts in childhood, has a limiting effect on the other components of fitness. High body fat is associated with a number of health problems including heart disease, high blood pressure, stroke, diabetes, cancer and back pain.

Did You Know?

Consistent resistance training 2–3 times a week can increase your resting metabolism about 100 kilocalories a day.

On Your Mark, Get Set . . . Wait!

It is always a good idea to undergo a medical examination before embarking on a strenuous program of exercise.

   With your physician, write up a personal medical profile including a history of high blood pressure, chest pain, heart arrhythmia, or shortness of breath. Determine your coronary heart disease risk. Here's a list of heart disease risk factors and what you can do about them.

RISK FACTOR	CRITERIA
Positive Risk Factors	
Family history	Myocardial infarction or sudden death before 55 years of age in father or other male first-degree relative (i.e., brother or son) or before 65 years of age in mother or female first-degree relative (i.e., sister or daughter)
Cigarette smoking	Current cigarette smoker or those who quit within previous 6 months
High blood pressure	Systolic blood pressure ≥ 140 mmHg or diastolic ≥ 90 mmHg (confirmed on two separate occasions) or taking antihypertensive medication
Hypercholesterolemia	Total serum cholesterol > 200 mg/dL, or high-density lipoprotein cholesterol < 40 mg/dL, or on lipid-lowering medication. If LDL-C is available, use > 130 mg/dL rather than total cholesterol.
Impaired fasting glucose	Fasting blood glucose of ≥ 110 mg/dL (confirmed on at least two separate occasions)
Obesity	Body Mass Index of ≥ 30 kg/m^2 or waist girth > 102 cm (40 inches) for men and > 88 cm (35 inches) for women or waist/hip ratio ≥ 0.95 for men and ≥ 0.86 for women
Sedentary lifestyle	Persons not participating in a regular exercise program or meeting the minimal physical activity recommendations from the U.S. Surgeon General's report (accumulating 30 minutes or more of moderate intensity [somewhat hard] physical activity on most days of the week)
Negative Risk Factor	
High serum HDL-C	> 60 mg/dL of high density lipoprotein cholesterol
Note: Positive risk factors PROMOTE disease whereas negative risk factors NEGATE disease	

Metabolic Syndrome

What Is Metabolic Syndrome?

One out of every five Americans has metabolic syndrome. This is a cluster of health irregularities that raise a person's risk of heart disease, stroke and type 2 diabetes considerably. How do you know if you have metabolic syndrome?

A person has metabolic syndrome if they have at least three of the following:

1. Fasting blood sugar of at least 110 mg/dL

2. Blood pressure of at least 130 mmHg (systolic) or 85 mmHg (diastolic) or both

3. Triglycerides of at least 150 mg/dL

4. HDL (healthy) cholesterol of less than 50 mg/dL for women or less than 40 mg/dL for men

5. A waist circumference greater than 35 inches for women or greater than 40 inches for men

How Can You Prevent Metabolic Syndrome?

Daily aerobic exercise of at least 30 accumulated minutes at a moderate intensity is recommended. If you are overweight, weight loss is very beneficial. Eating a heart healthy diet is also encouraged. This includes eating less saturated fat in your diet. Also, limit your consumption of butter, cheese, whole milk and ice cream. Eat more foods rich in healthy protein such as chicken, seafood, eggs, nuts, lean beef and beans.

In addition, eat more fresh fruits and vegetables and include more whole grain fiber containing foods, which have less of an impact on blood glucose levels. Select more polyunsaturated fats such as vegetable oils, salad dressings, nuts and fish foods. Lastly, try to avoid refined carbohydrates such as cakes and cookies.

Blood Pressure

Over 30 percent of Americans have high blood pressure (hypertension) and 25% have prehypertension (see more below). In fact, your lifetime risk of developing hypertension is close to 90 percent. This risk tends to rise with your chronological age. Controlling your blood pressure lowers the risk of stroke by 35 to 45 percent and the risk of heart attack by 20 to 25 percent! Almost 1/3 of the people with high blood pressure don't know they have it.

Tips to Help You Lower Your Blood Pressure (if above normal)

1. **Lose Extra Weight:** If overweight, for every 20 lbs. you lose there is a drop of about 5 to 20 points in your systolic blood pressure.

2. **Eat a Lower Fat Diet:** Choose more vegetables, fruits and low-fat dairy foods in your diet.

3. **Exercise Daily:** Shoot for at least 30 minutes of moderate intensity exercise on most days of the week. This can be continuous or accumulated minutes (i.e., such as three 10-minute walks during the day).

4. **Reduce Sodium Intake:** Eat no more than 2,400 mg of sodium per day with an optimal goal of keeping sodium intake to about 1,500 mg.

5. **Limit Alcohol Consumption:** If you do drink, have no more than two drinks per day for men and one for women. Examples of one drink are a 12-ounce beer, 5 ounces of wine, or 1.5 ounces of 80-proof whiskey.

TAKE NOTE: If your blood pressure varies a lot, make sure it is being measured correctly. You should be seated quietly for at least five minutes in a chair, feet on the floor, with your arm supported at the height of your heart. At least two measurements should be taken. Some persons have what is referred to as "office hypertension" or "white coat hypertension" which is a rise in blood pressure due to nervousness from just being at a doctor's office. If this is you, take some extra minutes to relax before measurements.

Category	Systolic		Diastolic
Normal	< 120 mmHg	AND	< 80 mmHg
Prehypertension	120–139 mmHg	OR	80–89 mmHg
Hypertension	≥ 140 mmHg	OR	≥ 90 mmHg

Note, when systolic and diastolic blood pressure fall into different categories, use the higher category.

From the Seventh Report of the Joint National Committee on Prevention, Detection, Evaluation, and Treatment of High Blood Pressure.

Diabetes Test Station: Beware the "Sugar Disease"!

Diabetes is the fastest growing disease in America. A total of 25.8 million children and adults have diabetes. Approximately 1.9 million new cases of diabetes are diagnosed each year. Alarmingly, 79 million people have pre-diabetes.

Fasting Blood Glucose Test (after a 12-hour fast)	
Normal	< 100 mg/dL
Pre-diabetes	≥ 100 mg/dL to < 126 mg/dL
Diabetes	≥ 126 mg/dL or higher
Oral Glucose Test (tested after drinking a glucose-laden drink)	
Normal	< 140 mg/dL
Pre-diabetes	≥ 140 mg/dL to < 200 mg/dL
Diabetes	≥ 200 mg/dL or higher

Type 1, or insulin-dependent diabetes mellitus (IDDM), usually occurs before the age of 30 although it can develop at any stage of life. Type 2, or non-insulin dependent diabetes mellitus (NIDDM), is more common with up to 95 percent of all cases. There is no cure for diabetes, but the best prevention/management plan is regular exercise and proper diet. With exercise, strive to accumulate 200 minutes of moderate intensity exercise throughout the week. With diet, cut back on all unhealthy fats such as those found in fried foods and buttered popcorn, and limit refined starches and sweets. Eat more vegetables, seafood, poultry, low-fat dairy foods, beans, vegetable oils, nuts, whole grain breads and cereals, and unsaturated fats. Four out of every five people with type 2 diabetes are over-weight, so weight loss is often recommended.

Take Note: Boosting your physical activity and losing excess weight are the best ways to avoid diabetes.

How Fit Are You?

Here are some simple self-assessment tests to help determine or monitor your level of fitness. Periodically retest yourself to monitor your progress. STOP if you feel any nausea, discomfort, dizziness, or breathlessness. Perform the test on another day.

Aerobic Efficiency

Step Test

1. Select a bench, stool, or chair that is 12 inches high.

2. You will step up and down in an up, up, down, down brisk cadence.

3. Find a song that has a moderate tempo of about 96 beats per minute (16 beats in 10 seconds) to guide your cadence.

4. Rehearse stepping with the music to become familiar with the pattern.

5. Practice finding your pulse on your wrist (on the inner edge of the wrist below the base of the thumb) or at your neck (below the ear along the jaw).

6. Now, perform the stepping for three continuous minutes. On completion of the time, immediately count your pulse for 10 seconds.

7. Record score and rating in the *Student Profile Guide* on page 11.

STEP TEST RATING (COUNTING PULSE FOR 10 SECONDS)			
Level	**Women**	**Men**	
Excellent	16 or less	17 or less	Congratulations!
Good	17–18	18–20	Keep it up!
Fair	19–22	21–23	Begin or progress in an aerobic program.
Poor	23 or more	24 or more	Start with a moderate to easy aerobic program.
(Test based on the Harvard Step Test.)			

1.5-Mile Run Test

1. Establish a distance of 1.5 miles. This is six laps around most school tracks (which are usually one-quarter mile).

2. Use a stopwatch to time yourself.

3. Warm up with some easy jogging and gentle stretching before you start.

4. Cover the distance as fast as you can (running/walking). Cool down gradually at the conclusion with brisk walking for several minutes.

5. Record score and rating in the *Student Profile Guide* on page 12.

RATING THE 1.5-MILE RUN TIME (MINUTES)							
		Age (years)					
Fitness Category		**13–19**	**20–29**	**30–39**	**40–49**	**50–59**	**60+**
I. Very poor	(men)	>15:31*	>16:01	>16:31	>17:31	>19:01	>20:01
	(women)	>18:31	>19:01	>19:31	>20:01	>20:31	>21:01
II. Poor	(men)	12:11–15:30	14:01–16:00	14:44–16:30	15:36–17:30	17:01–19:00	19:01–20:00
	(women)	16:55–18:30	18:31–19:00	19:01–19:30	19:01–20:00	20:01–20:30	21:00–21:31
III. Fair	(men)	10:49–12:10	12:01–14:00	12:31–14:45	13:01–15:35	14:31–17:00	16:16–19:00
	(women)	14:31–16:54	15:55–18:30	16:31–19:00	17:31–19:30	19:01–20:00	19:31–20:30
IV. Good	(men)	9:41–10:48	10:46–12:00	11:01–12:30	11:31–13:00	12:31–14:30	14:00–16:15
	(women)	12:30–14:30	13:31–15:54	14:31–16:30	15:56–17:30	16:31–19:00	17:31–19:30
V. Excellent	(men)	8:37–9:40	9:45–10:45	10:00–11:00	10:30–11:30	11:00–12:30	11:15–13:59
	(women)	11:50–12:29	12:30–13:30	13:00–14:30	13:45–15:55	14:30–16:30	16:30–17:30
VI. Superior	(men)	<8:37	<9:45	<10:00	<10:30	<11:00	<11:15
	(women)	<11:50	<12:30	<13:00	<13:45	<14:30	<16:30

< Means "less than"; > means "more than."

"1.5 mile run tests," from *The Aerobics Program for Total Well Being* by Kenneth H. Cooper M.D., M.P.H, Copyright © 1982 by Kenneth H. Cooper. Used by permission of Bantam Books, a division of Bantam Double-day Dell Publishing Group, Inc.

Rockport Fitness Walking Test

The Rockport Walking Institute has developed a walking test to assess maximal cardiorespiratory fitness (VO_2max) for men and women. It is helpful to do this test with a workout partner. Classes often do this test in two groups. A heart rate monitor (if available) and a watch are needed for this aerobic test.

1. Find a 1-mile course that is flat, uninterrupted, and correctly measured. A quarter-mile track is preferable for the outdoors.

2. Walk 1 mile as quickly and comfortably as possible and have your workout partner record your time at the finish mark to the closest second. For example, if a person finishes in 13 minutes and 35 seconds, the time is converted to the nearest hundredth minute by dividing the seconds (35) by 60 seconds. Thus, the time is 13.55 minutes.

3. If using a heart rate monitor, get your heart rate the instant you cross the 1-mile mark. If taking a pulse, upon crossing the finish mark immediately take a heart rate by counting your pulse for 15 seconds. Multiply that number by four to get your heart rate for one minute.

4. You can also do this test inside, especially during unpleasant weather. Walk 1 mile as fast as you can by adjusting the speed of the treadmill. Make sure you do not jog or run and keep the treadmill grade at 0% for the test. Record the time from the computer display and take your heart rate with a heart rate monitor or by taking your pulse.

5. Calculate your VO_2max using the following equation.

6. VO_2max (ml/kg/min) = 132.853 − (0.0769 × weight) − (0.3877 × age) + (6.315 × gender) − (3.2649 × time) − (0.1565 × heart rate)

   Where:

   a. Time is expressed in minutes and 100ths of a minute
   b. Weight is in pounds (lbs)
   c. Gender Male = 1 and Female = 0
   d. Heart rate is in beats/minute
   e. Age is in years

Example VO₂max Calculations for a Female and Male:

For a 22-year-old Female who weighs 140 lbs who completed the Rockport Walk Test in 13 minutes and 35 seconds, or 13.55 minutes, with a heart rate of 150 beats per minute the calculation would be as follows:

$$132.853 - (0.0769 \times 140) - (0.3877 \times 22) + (6.315 \times 0) - (3.2649 \times 13.55) - (0.1565 \times 150)$$

$$VO_2max \ (ml/kg/min) = 45.73 \ ml/kg/min$$

For a 22-year-old Male who weighs 140 lbs who completed the Rockport Walk Test in 13 minutes and 35 seconds, or 13.55 minutes, with a heart rate of 150 beats per minute the calculation would be as follows:

$$132.853 - (0.0769 \times 140) - (0.3877 \times 22) + (6.315 \times 1) - (3.2649 \times 13.55) - (0.1565 \times 150)$$

$$VO_2max \ (ml/kg/min) = 52.05 \ ml/kg/min$$

Use the charts below to classify your cardiorespiratory fitness.

7. Record score and rating in the *Student Profile Guide* on page 14.

MALES: CARDIORESPIRATORY FITNESS CLASSIFICATION: VO₂MAX (ML/KG/MIN)						
Age	Superior	Excellent	Very Good	Good	Fair	Poor
20–30	>60	54–59	48–53	45–47	37–44	≤36
31–40	>56	50–55	45–49	39–44	34–38	≤33
41–50	>50	46–49	40–45	36–39	30–35	≤29
51–60	>46	42–45	37–41	33–36	28–32	≤27

FEMALES: CARDIORESPIRATORY FITNESS CLASSIFICATION: VO₂MAX (ML/KG/MIN)						
Age	Superior	Excellent	Very Good	Good	Fair	Poor
20–30	>50	46–49	42–45	36–41	32–35	≤31
31–40	>46	42–45	38–41	33–37	28–32	≤27
41–50	>41	38–40	34–37	28–33	25–27	≤24
51–60	>37	32–36	29–31	26–28	22–25	≤21

Tables derived from graphs by Shvartz, E. and Reibold, R.C. Aerobic fitness norms for males and females aged 6 to 75 years: A review. Aviation, Space, and Environmental Medicine, 61, 3–11

Muscular Strength and Endurance

Abdominal Strength and Endurance Test

1. Lie on your back with your hands either supporting your head or across your chest.

2. Keep your legs bent at the knees, with the feet flat on the floor about 6 to 10 inches from your buttocks.

3. To perform the "crunch," curl your trunk so that your shoulder blades come off the floor. (Your lower back stays on the floor.) Keep the movements smooth.

4. To take the test, count the number of "crunches" you can do for one minute.

5. Record results and rating in the *Student Profile Guide* on page 15.

RATING FOR ABDOMINAL STRENGTH AND ENDURANCE TEST	
Category	**Results**
Excellent	60 crunches or more
Very Good	50 to 59 crunches
Good	42 to 49 crunches
Fair	34 to 41 crunches
Poor	Less than 34 crunches

Upper Torso Strength and Endurance Test

The push-up test measures upper-body endurance, specifically in the chest (pectoralis muscles), shoulder (anterior deltoids) and arms (triceps). Due to common variations in upper body strength, women should be assessed doing the modified push-up. Men should be assessed using the standard push-up. However, as the illustration shows, for training women should do either the standard or modified push-up depending on which provides the optimal challenge.

1. The start position is with the chest lowered so it almost makes contact with the floor. Extend the arms on the upward phase.

2. To take the test, count the total number of push-ups completed in one minute.

3. Record results and rating in the *Student Profile Guide* on page 15.

PUSH-UP TEST NORMS FOR MODIFIED PUSH-UP (WOMEN)					
AGE	Excellent	Good	Average	Poor	Very Poor
20–29	>48	34–48	17–33	6–16	<6
30–39	>39	25–39	12–24	4–11	<4
40–49	>34	20–34	8–19	3–7	<3
50–59	>29	15–29	6–14	2–5	<2

PUSH-UP TEST NORMS (MEN)					
AGE	Excellent	Good	Average	Poor	Very Poor
20–29	>54	45–54	35–44	20–34	<20
30–39	>44	35–44	24–34	15–23	<15
40–49	>39	30–39	20–29	12–19	<12
50–59	>34	25–34	15–24	8–14	<8

Norms for men and women adapted from Pollock, M.L. et al. *Health and Fitness Through Physical Activity*, New York: John Wiley & Sons.

Flexibility

Sit-and-Reach Test

Flexibility is specific. This means that the degree of flexibility in one joint will not necessarily be the same in other joints of the body. Because a lack of flexibility in the lower back, back of the legs, and hips is a contributing cause for 80 percent of the low back pain in the U.S. adult population, this flexibility test was chosen.

1. Sit with your legs extended in front of you. Keep your feel perpendicular to the floor. Place a ruler along your legs on the floor.

2. Slowly stretch forward, reaching toward (or past) your toes and hold. (Do not bounce!) Keep your legs straight but not locked.

3. It is best to do this several times for practice, gently stretching further toward your point of limitation.

4. Record results and rating in the *Student Profile Guide* on page 17.

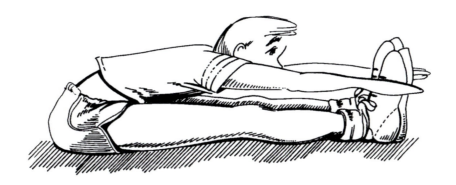

RATINGS FOR THE SIT-AND-REACH TEST	
Category	**Results**
Excellent	7 inches or more past the toes
Very Good	4 to 7 inches past the toes
Good	1 to 4 inches past the toes
Fair	2 inches from in front of the toes to 1 inch past
Poor	More than 2 inches in front of the toes
A limitation of this sit-and-reach test is that it does not differentiate between a person with short arms and/or long legs and someone with long arms and/or short legs. However, this test is appropriate to monitor flexibility changes over time.	

Body Composition

Pinch Test for Body Fat

The pinch test is a quick check for body composition. (You can always count on the mirror to tell you a lot, too!)

1. With your thumb and forefinger, pinch the skin and fat at the waist just above the hips. (Be sure not to pinch any muscle. Pull the skinfold away from your body.)

2. With a ruler measure the width of the pinch.

3. Record results and rating in the *Student Profile Guide* on page 18.

RATINGS FOR PINCH TEST		
Level	**Men**	**Women**
Good to Excellent	1/2 inch or less	1 inch or less
Fair to Good	1 inch to 1/2	1 1/2 inch to 1 inch
Poor	Over 1 inch	Over 1 1/2 inch
Refer to Skinfold Caliper Measurement for a more accurate estimate of body composition.		

Skinfold Caliper Measurement

Approximately one-third of the fat in the body is located just under the skin and is closely correlated to total body fat. Researchers have demonstrated that this skinfold fat is distributed differently in men and women and, for that reason, skinfold measurements are taken at different body locations. Skinfolds should not be taken immediately after exercise, because the shift of body fluids will increase the skinfold size.

There are several practical and inexpensive skinfold calipers available for body composition analysis. To take a skinfold measurement,

1. Grasp the anatomical site with the thumb and index finger.

2. Lift the skinfold away from the site to make sure no muscle is caught in the fold.

3. Place the caliper one-half inch below the thumb and index finger.

4. Allow the caliper to stabilize for a few seconds before reading. Take at least three measurements, and record the average.

5. Total the average of your skinfolds.

6. Determine your percentage of body fat by placing a straightedge from your age to the sum of the three skinfolds on the nomogram. The recommended percentage of body fat is 16 to 28 percent for a woman (18–34 years) and 5 to 15 percent for a man (18–34 years). There is an error factor of plus or minus 3 to 5 percent with skinfold body composition assessment.

7. Record the results and rating in the *Student Profile Guide* on page 18.

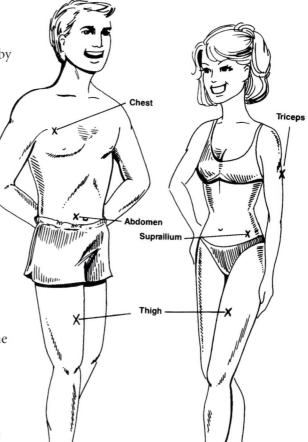

Anatomical Skinfold Sites

Skinfolds are conventionally taken on the right side of the body. Here is how to find the anatomical skinfold sites:

▶ **Chest**—the fold over the side border of the pectoralis major

▶ **Abdomen**—vertical fold adjacent to the umbilicus

▶ **Thigh**—vertical fold on the front part of the thigh midway between the hip and knee joint

▶ **Triceps**—vertical fold on the back of the arm midway between the shoulder and elbow (arm held straight and relaxed)

▶ **Suprailium**—diagonal fold above the crest of the ilium

Skinfold Nomogram

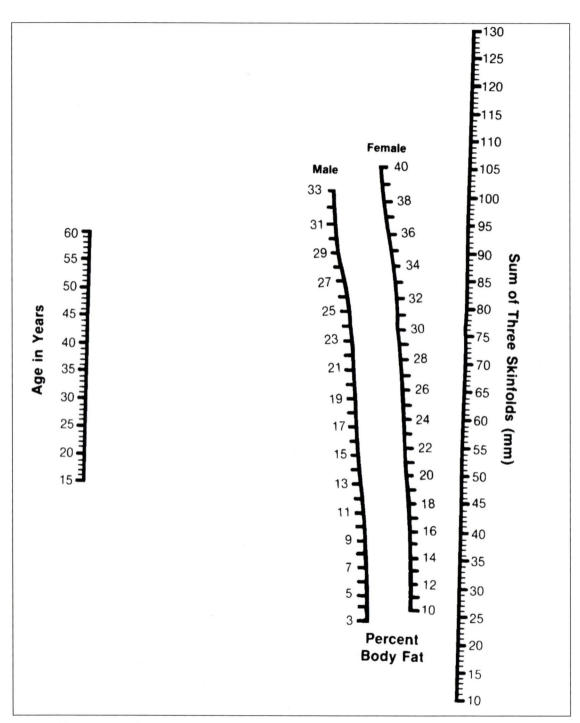

Reprinted by permission from Baun, W. B., Baun, M. R. A Nomogram for the Estimate of Percent Body Fat from Generalized Equations. *Research Quarterly for Exercise and Sport,* 52 (1981), 380–384.

The "S.P.O.R.T." Principle

Fitness conditioning involves the "S.P.O.R.T." principle: Specificity, Progression, Overload, Reversibility, and Training Effect.

Specificity: Specificity takes the guesswork out of training. Your body will adapt to the specific type of training you choose. If you want to run marathons, you've got to train long distances. If you wish to build muscles, you must do intense weight training. Identify your goals and get started.

Progression: Challenge your body's abilities gradually and regularly. Let your body adapt to its new capability, and then you can progress some more. (Injuries happen from trying to do too much, too soon, too hard, and too fast.)

Overload: You "overload" by increasing the intensity, duration, or frequency of your established level of exercise. For instance, you may do aerobics longer, more times a week, or at a more intense level. When your exercise program becomes easier and somewhat routine, it is often a good time to overload. Overload your exercise program in increments of about 5 percent of your present ability.

Reversibility: You can't store the benefits of exercise. If you stop exercising there will be a marked decrease in skill, endurance, and strength from your previous level. So keep it up!

Training Effect: As you specifically train for a certain activity, you gradually and progressively improve your body's fitness capacity. The resulting increase in muscular and cardiorespiratory conditioning is the training effect.

Your final phase is to **MAINTAIN** this newly acquired level of health throughout your lifetime. You can do it!

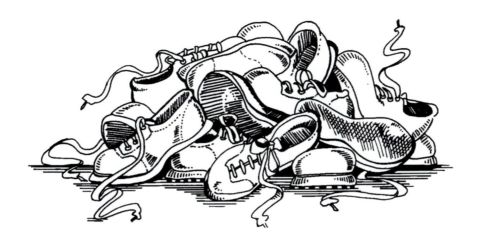

The Formula for Aerobic Fitness

To benefit from a sound cardiorespiratory program, follow the "F.I.T." formula. "F.I.T." stands for Frequency, Intensity, and Time.

Frequency: For optimal results, perform your aerobic activity three to five times a week (preferably every other day). If you choose to exercise more, make sure you rest at least one day each week to prevent any injuries from overuse!

Intensity: Your intensity should be 50 percent to 85 percent of your personalized training zone. For beginners in good health, 60 percent to 70 percent of your training zone is encouraged.

Time: The time or duration should gradually build up to between 20 and 60 minutes of continuous or intermittent activity (10 minute bouts accumulated throughout the day).

Did You Know?

Only 16 percent of all adults exercise regularly enough to promote health-related fitness.

Heart Rate Monitoring

Monitoring your heart rate is a very simple, practical, and safe way to understand your exertion during aerobics. You will improve your cardiorespiratory system if you train at 60 percent to 85 percent of your personalized target zone. To estimate your target zone, you must first calculate

PERSONALIZED TARGET ZONE WITH A 30-YEAR-OLD PERSON		
Your Estimated Maximum Heart Rate (MHR)	208 − (0.7 x Age in Years) = 187	
Your resting heart rate	−72	
Subtract resting heart rate from estimated MHR	115	
Multiply by	60%	85%
Equals	69	98
Add resting heart rate	+72	+72
Equals exercise heart rate	141	170
	Target Zone	

PERSONALIZED TARGET ZONE		
Your Estimated Maximum Heart Rate (MHR)	208 – (0.7 x Age in Years)	
Your resting heart rate		
Subtract resting heart rate from estimated MHR		
Multiply by	60%	85%
Equals		
Add resting heart rate		
Equals exercise heart rate		
	Target Zone	

your maximum heart rate and your resting heart rate. Your maximum heart rate (the fastest your heart will beat) can be estimated with the equation 208 – (0.7 × Age in Years). Resting heart rate is defined as the average heart rate (per minute) prior to initiating any physical activity. It is often measured in the morning, after waking up, and prior to physical activity. Here's how a 30-year-old individual with a resting heart rate of 72 would estimate her/his personalized target zone.

1. Find your pulse with your index and middle fingers pressed gently on your wrist (on the inner edge of the wrist below the base of the thumb) or neck (below the ear along the jaw) and count for 10 seconds.

2. Multiply by 6 to find the beats per minute. Pulse monitoring at the wrist is recommended because you can inadvertently press too hard on the neck and cause a slowing of the heart rate.

3. Monitor your heart rate before, after three to five minutes of aerobic exercise, and on completion of an aerobic section. Keep moving while you take your exercise pulse.

Some students find it easy to calculate their personalized target zone for a 10-second count. To do this, divide your exercise heart rate by 6. For instance, if your personalized target zone is 150 beats per minute to 180 beats per minute, your 10-second count would be determined as follows: 150/6 = 25; 180/6 = 30. So, if you do a 10-second pulse check while exercising, your heart rate should be between 25 and 30.

Perceived Exertion

You can also monitor exercise intensity through the use of perceived exertion. With perceived exertion, you interpret various body sensations such as heart rate, muscle and joint sensations, breathing intensity, and body temperature, and subjectively estimate your exercise intensity. A model that corresponds exercise heart rate with perceived exertion has been developed by Gunnar Borg, a Swedish physiologist. Notice that by adding a "0" to the numbers of the perceived exertion scale, it correlates to your exercise heart rate intensity. This is a great way to learn to listen to your body and compare your results to your counted heart rate. The American College of Sports Medicine recommends training in the 12 to 16 range of the perceived exertion scale to improve your aerobic capacity.

Talk Test

A very easy and accurate way to know if you are in your optimal aerobic training intensity is to perform the 'talk test'. If you can cite the 'Pledge of Allegiance' (or any 35 word phrase) with mild difficulty while doing your aerobic workout you are probably in the desired aerobic exercise intensity range.

Finding Your Pulse

Rate of Perceived Exertion Scale

6	
7	Very, very light
8	
9	Very light
10	
11	Fairly light
12	
13	Somewhat hard
14	
15	Hard
16	
17	Very hard
18	
19	Very, very hard
20	

From Borg, G. "Perceived Exertion: A Note on History and Methods." *Medicine and Science in Sports and Exercise* 5:90–93, 1983.

All about Strength, Function, and Core

Strength is the ability to overcome a resistance. Several studies have shown the health benefits of strength training to include the following in many persons:

- increased muscle mass
- increased bone mineral density
- improved glucose metabolism
- improved blood lipid levels
- reduced lower-back pain
- reduced arthritic pain
- improved gastrointestinal transit
- maintained metabolic rate during weight loss interventions

> **Did You Know?**
>
> People with high levels of muscular strength have lower incidences of chronic diseases such as diabetes, stroke, arthritis, and heart disease.

Your overall strength is determined by numerous factors, including the intensity of training you regularly do, the predominant muscle fiber type of your muscles, hormonal levels, tendon insertion points, body proportions, and neurological efficiency. Here are some key terms and concepts to know about strength training.

A **concentric muscle action** (or contraction) describes a muscle going through a shortening motion as it overcomes the resistance.

During **eccentric muscle actions** (or contractions), the muscle lengthens as it resists the load. So, if you examine a person doing a biceps curl exercise, the upward phase of the movement is the concentric action, and the lowering phase of the movement is the eccentric action.

An **isometric action** (or contraction) is the amount of strength an individual can exhibit at a single point in the range of motion. With isometric actions, there is no limb movement or change in the joint angle. Just holding a weight in one position is an example of isometric strength.

Speed strength is a term that is interchangeable with the term power. Speed strength refers to the maximum force exhibited over a distance at a certain speed of movement. Examples of speed strength in sports include throwing a javelin and striking a punching bag.

Absolute strength is the maximal amount of weight that an individual can lift at one time. It is sometimes referred to as the one-repetition maximum, abbreviated IRM.

Relative strength is a useful method for comparing the strength between different individuals. It is the ratio of the amount weight lifted to total body weight. For example, if a person can do a one repetition maximum biceps curl with 50 lbs. and weighs 130 lbs., what is the relative strength for this muscle group? To solve, set up a ratio and compute: 50 lbs./130 lbs. = .38. Relative strength is reported as a percentage, so multiplying by 100 will make this answer 38 percent for the relative strength of the biceps muscles.

Functional strength is a very popular term now used in fitness and sports. In fitness, functional strength applies to doing exercises that will enhance a person's ability to execute everyday activities. Some professionals also use the term **meaningful exercise** to describe functional strength. With functional strength, exercises are chosen that are task-specific to help a person perform better in daily life. Numerous exercises throughout this text offer significant functional strength benefits.

In sports, functional strength is used to enhance an athlete's sports performance. For recreational and competitive athletes, trainers and coaches try to duplicate the range of motion (or a portion of the range) with an exercise. For instance, a push-up is excellent for developing the strength of the shoulder joint, yet not the best functional exercise choice for training a golfer. When working with a golfer, the trainer might design an exercise that goes through more of a diagonal pathway, such as the motion of swinging a golf club.

Core strength or core stability training is a relatively new type of strength training in the health and fitness industry. Core training involves exercises that strengthen the deep spinal muscles. These are the deep abdominal and lower back muscles surrounding the spine, often referred to as the intrinsic muscles. The purpose of core training is to spare the spine from damage. Stability training creates a stable and mobile lower back. Development of core strength leads to a greater enjoyment of exercise participation and improvement in exercise performance. Several exercises in this text have been included to improve core strength.

How Do Muscles Grow?

Muscle growth, which is called muscle hypertrophy, is of great interest to many exercise enthusiasts. Many types of resistance training will help a person develop muscle hypertrophy. With muscle hypertrophy there is an increase in the muscle fiber size. The muscle attains a larger diameter. New muscle fibers are not created, although this occurrence has been observed in some animal studies. With muscle hypertrophy in people, the contractile proteins within the muscle increase in size and number. In addition, there is an increase in the fluid (called sarcoplasm) region of the muscle.

It is important to note that strength gains that occur the first couple of months of any resistance training program are primarily neural adaptations. In the early training phases of resistance training the muscle is acquiring greater input signals from the nerves, referred to as neural drive.

What Training Methods Promote Muscle Growth?

Some of the following body building training methods promote muscle growth.

Descending Weight Sets or Drop Sets

Here is an example of doing descending weight sets or drop sets. An exerciser may do 8 repetitions of dumbbell lateral raises with 30 lbs to momentary muscular fatigue (MMF), where she/he can't do another repetition, and then put the dumbbells down and complete 8 repetitions with 25 lbs to MMF and then drop to 8 repetitions of 20 lbs to MMF. A sequential drop of 10–25% in weight would be appropriate with this technique.

Eccentric Training

With eccentric training the exercisers lifts the weight in 1 second and lowers the weight in 3–4 seconds. One popular eccentric training technique is the 'supramaximal technique,' where the exercise enthusiast lifts a weight (with the aid of a workout partner or personal trainer) that is 105% to 120% of their normal weight and then lowers the weight slowly in 3–4 seconds.

Forced Repetitions

With the spotting aid of a workout partner or personal trainer, complete 2–4 extra repetitions after reaching MMF on a set.

Super Sets

Super sets are any two sets that are performed in sequence (with no rest between exercises). Possible super set strategies (and examples of each) include agonist/antagonist (biceps curl and triceps extension), opposite action (chest fly and seated row), upper body/lower body (chest press and leg press), lower body only (lunge and heel raise) and upper body only (fly and chest press).

The Ten Commandments of Strength Training

Doing your exercises is not enough. It's doing them right that really counts. Follow these 10 commandments for effective results.

1. **Control your movement.** Avoid fast, jerky movements that rely too heavily on momentum and may be harmful to your muscles and joints. A safe recommendation for resistance exercise is to perform the ascending motion for two seconds and the descending motion for four seconds.

2. **Perform all exercises through the complete range of motion.** The benefits of strength, endurance, flexibility, skill, and performance are best achieved when exercises are performed through the full range of movement. Sometimes small range-of-motion movements are incorporated with the full range movements. (Exception: to avoid stressing the neck, do not take the head straight back.)

3. **Always exercise opposing muscle groups.** You need to balance the strength of opposing muscles. (See THE MUSCLE SYSTEM for a list of opposing muscle groups.)

4. **Concentrate on the muscles you are working.** Focusing on the specific muscle groups you are working will help you know when and how much to overload.

5. **Do the exercises properly.** The quality, form, and technique of the exercise is very important. Don't just try to see how many repetitions of an exercise you can do!

6. **Breathe normally.** Always exhale as you exert. Do not hold your breath!

7. **Don't exercise to the point of pain.** Pain is a warning sign—STOP before you hurt yourself. For optimal results, challenge yourself to the point of momentary muscular fatigue to sufficiently overload the muscles.

8. **Vary your program and exercises.** This prevents boredom, staleness, and overtraining.

9. **Exercise major body parts early in the workout.** Work your larger muscle groups, such as your legs and chest, before isolating your smaller muscle groups. That way the fatigue in the smaller muscle groups will not affect the performance of the heavier, more-difficult exercises.

10. **Be faithful to your warm-up and cooldown routines.** The warm-up prepares the body for the workout to follow and helps to decrease the risk of injury. It should include low-intensity movements very similar to the workout activity. The cooldown helps the body recover toward a normal resting level. Stretching exercises are recommended to help promote mind and body relaxation and to prevent muscle soreness.

SECTION 2

TRAINING TIPS AND INJURY PREVENTION

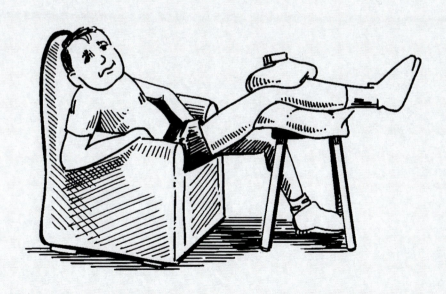

Maximize Your Results, Minimize Your Risks

Not all exercises are good for you. Here are some unsafe or poorly executed exercises with their preferred alternatives.

1. **Twisting Hops** The combination of twisting the spine while hopping on the floor can be quite stressful on the back. The force of hopping alone equals two to three times your body weight.

   Alternative: Jump rope hops do not require any twisting and are more controllable.

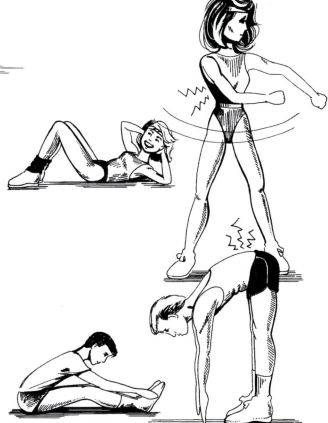

2. **Fast-Twisting Waist Exercises** The fast side-to-side twisting of the torso imposes a shearing stress on the vertebrae of the spine.

   Alternative: Do them slowly as a warm-up stretch. Twisting crunches are more effective waist work.

3. **Toe Touches** The straight-legged toe touch position stretches the ligaments behind the knees too much and stresses the lower spine. Bouncing touches are even worse!

   Alternative: The seated pike stretch (with slightly bent knees) and the seated half-straddle stretch are much better for you.

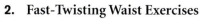

4. **Windmill Stretch** This stretch also places too much stress on the ligaments supporting the spine. The twist adds stress to your back.
   Alternative: Try a seated side straddle stretch for greater control and safety.

5. **Ballet Barre Leg Stretches**
   Any person with back problems may inadvertently overstretch the sciatic nerve beyond its normal range.

   Alternative: The single-leg hamstring stretch on the back and the seated half-straddle are recommended alternatives.

6. **Deep Knee Bends** Deep knee bend variations can overstretch the ligaments supporting the knee and compress the cartilage.
   Alternative: When squatting, keep the knees from protruding past the toes, and lower your buttocks to just above your knees.

7. **Lunges with Protruding Knees** The lunge is often incorrectly performed. A bent knee that juts past the ankle places stress on the knee.

Alternative: Make sure the front knee stays over the toes.

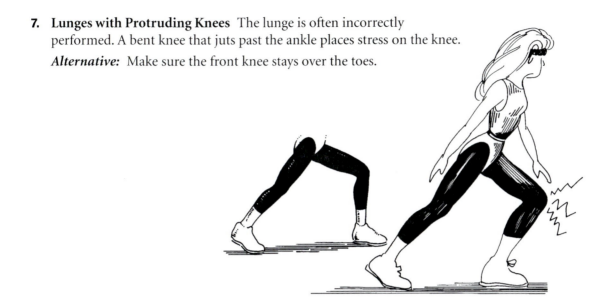

8. **Hurdler's Stretch** This exercise can overstretch the muscles in the groin and the ligaments of the bent knee.

Alternative: The seated center straddle stretch and half-straddle stretch are better options.

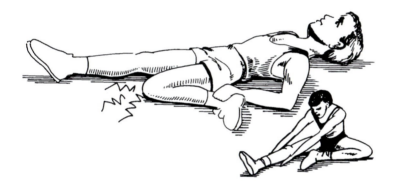

9. **Sit-ups with Straight Legs, Anchored Feet, Double Leg Lifts, or Jackknife Sit-ups** These exercises predominantly use the hip flexors (the muscles in front of the thigh that attach to the lower back), not the abdominals! Their repeated performance may lead to low back discomfort and pain.

Alternative: Use the "crunch" variations that bring your ribs toward your pelvis as you lift only your shoulders and upper back off the floor. See pages 83 and 84.

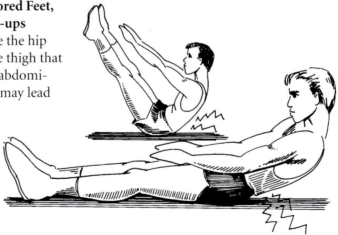

10. **Head Throws in a Crunch** Often the head is "thrown forward" during a crunch.

    Alternative: Keep your head in a neutral or normal position. Focus on the ceiling when performing this exercise.

11. **Swan Lifts** The combination of arching the lower spine as the muscles are contracting can injure the back.

    Alternative: Keep the lower body on the floor and only lift the upper body, as in the back extension. Or, simultaneously lift one arm in front while lifting the opposite leg in back. Repeat the movement lifting the opposite limbs.

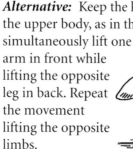

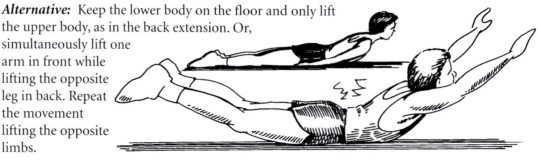

12. **The Plow** This movement places too much stress on the discs and bones of the neck. It may inhibit breathing and blood flow.

    Alternative: The seated pike stretch (with soft knees) is safer.

13. **Gymnastics Bridges and Pelvic Lifts** The gymnastics bridge, designed to stretch the upper back and shoulders, is usually performed with an overarched lower back. Pelvic lifts are frequently overarched as well.

    Alternative: Use the prone prop or prone extension instead of the bridge (See page 45). And be careful not to overarch when performing the pelvic lift.

14. **Leg Lifting Exercises** Leg lifts or side leg exercises can twist and strain the lower back if they are done too fast.

    Alternative: Place your elbows on the floor, keep your back straight, and control the movement. Do not swing or fling legs.

15. **Needle Point Exercise** Unless you have great flexibility and control, the needle point exercise places abnormal stress on the lower back and the back of the supporting knee.

    Alternative: Regular leg lifts from the elbows and knees are safer and just as effective.

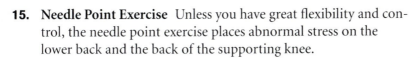

16. **Side Straddle Stretch** If you allow the opposite hip to come off the floor while stretching to the side, you place the hip and spine in poor alignment.

    Alternative: Keep the buttocks and legs firmly on the floor.

17. **Neck Extensions and 360-Degree Head Rolls** Taking the head straight back, as in neck extensions or full head rolls, may place too much stress on the disks of the neck vertebrae.

    Alternative: Neck rotation and lateral flexion are much safer. It is okay to bring the head forward and back, but avoid taking it too far past its neutral position when moving posteriorly.

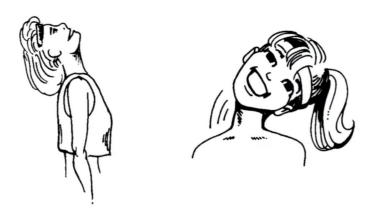

Twelve Most Common Exercise Mistakes

The following are some of the most common mistakes that occur in exercise programs.

1. **Overtraining** In their zeal to achieve fitness, people often try too hard. Possible signs of overtraining are injury, weight loss, mental dullness, disturbed digestion, loss of appetite, early exhaustion during a workout, fatigue during the day, or elevated heart rate upon awakening in the morning, or after a workout. Stress quality, not quantity!

2. **Poor Exercise Technique** Exercises performed incorrectly can lead to injury and poor performance. Poor technique is most frequent during the latter stages of a workout, when fatigue is starting to occur.

3. **Improper Equipment** The exercise clothes you wear, the shoes on your feet, the surface you are training on, and the equipment you are using can all **improve** or **impair** your performance.

4. **Insufficient Warm-up** Too often, the main activity is begun without proper warm-up (or after a quick, insufficient warm-up). This can lead to injury.

5. **Extra-Long Workouts** See signs of overtraining.

6. **Lifting Weights That Are Too Heavy**
This leads to improper exercise technique, predisposes you to injury, and is not the progressive overload needed for optimal results in strength and endurance. Realize your limits.

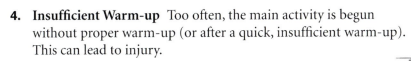

7. **Forgetting Muscle Groups** For complete body symmetry make sure you work **all** your muscle groups.

8. **Unrealistic Goal Setting** Set realistic short- and long-term goals.

9. **Forced Breathing** Proper breathing during exercise is easy to remember—**exhale** as you **exert.** Do not force your breathing.

10. **Exercises That Are Too Bouncy and Fast** Fast and bouncy movements stimulate your opposing muscle groups to contract and hinder the movement. Control is the key!

11. **Inadequate Aerobic Cooldown** Blood pressure may drop significantly from an abrupt cessation of vigorous aerobic exercise. This may also lead to fainting and irregular heart beats. Slow down gradually; don't just stop!

12. **Insufficient Stretching at the End of the Workout** Slow stretching following a workout helps reduce muscle soreness and improve flexibility.

Did You Know?

55% of people drop out of exercise within the first year of starting.

Did You Know?

The largest muscle in the human body is the gluteus maximus.

Injuries

In Case of Injury

Let's face it, when you pursue an active lifestyle you will occasionally overdo it. And even if you are careful, inadequate equipment or exercising on an improper surface can lead to injuries. You can usually tell when you have an injury; pain and swelling appear in an area and gradually worsen. What do you do? R.I.C.E. (Rest, Ice, Compression, Elevation) is the answer. Most of these problems are muscle, ligament, and tendon injuries. The R.I.C.E. approach will limit the injury and accelerate the healing.

Rest:
Rest prevents you from reinjury and decreases the circulation to the area. "Time heals."

Ice:
Ice should be applied immediately to the injured area to keep the swelling down. An ice pack may be applied for 10 to 20 minutes periodically through the first 24 hours. Direct ice massage can be used for 7- to 10-minute sessions with the same effects. Heat can be applied after 48 hours, in conjunction with ice, to increase the circulation and enhance the body's process of removing the excess blood and fluid.

Compression:
Compression helps reduce the swelling and internal bleeding. Ace bandages are a good way to do this. Be careful not to obstruct circulation by overtightening!

Elevation:
Elevation helps reduce the internal bleeding and excessive fluid entry to the injury. If possible, elevate the injured area above the level of the heart at all opportune times until the swelling subsides.

See your physician if necessary. Persistent pain, major swelling, and significant discoloration all require elevation. The **cause** of the injury must also be **corrected** so reinjury does not occur. (Maybe you need new shoes, less weight, shorter workouts, etc.) Begin your rehabilitation process of stretching and strengthening and return to your former level of activity when your body is READY!

Common Aerobic Injuries

Shin Splints

The most common aerobic injury is a pain between the knee and ankle, commonly referred to as "shin splints." Shin pain can be caused by a number of conditions, but impact shock is probably the major cause. Rest, ice, and exercise to increase muscle strength/flexibility are standard treatments. Footwear (specifically the arch support), floor surface resiliency, movement selection, and the structure of the workout should be reevaluated for safety and effectiveness. If this pain continues, see your physician.

Knee Injuries

A variety of knee injuries that affect the joint structure may also occur from repeated impact forces of aerobic exercise. Proper footwear, resilient workout surface, sufficient warm-up, and the progressive increase in exercise intensity will help to prevent these injuries.

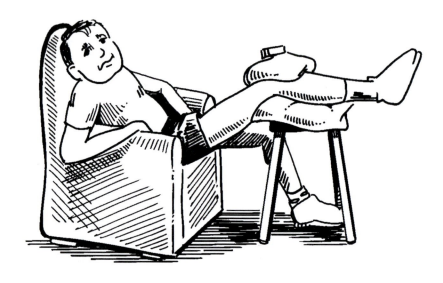

Ankle Sprain

An ankle sprain is the most common of all injuries. It usually occurs when the weak ligaments on the outside of the joint are injured by an accidental rolling outward of the ankle. Rest, ice, compression, and elevation are standard treatments; physician referral may be necessary. Safe movement selection, proper warm-up, and concentration on the activity itself will help prevent this type of injury.

Muscle and Ligament Inflammation

Another common injury that occurs from the repeated impact of the foot striking the ground is an inflammation of the muscles and ligaments supporting the foot. Overtraining and improper warm-up often lead to this ailment. Rest, ice, compression, and elevation are recommended treatments. Proper footwear and safe training procedures are preventives.

Guide to a Better Back

It's a pain! Why do you get this lower-back pain and what can you do to prevent back problems? Although there may be a number of different contributing factors to low back pain, it's essential to realize that when you stand upright, most of your body weight falls on the lower back. Weak abdominal and back muscles from underuse and/or poor posture may not give the spine the support it needs, leaving the back prone to pain or injury. Your goal to a healthy back is to keep the muscles of the spine, buttocks, and upper legs strong and flexible, be aware of preferred posture, and control your weight.

Healthy Back Tips

Standing and Walking

Maintain your normal back curve, but avoid the swayback posture. Stand tall, feeling lifted throughout the lower abdominal region. Try not to stand still too long. If you must, put one leg up on a support or at least bend alternate knees. Ladies, limit your high heel wearing time because these shoes accentuate the back curve and create stress on the spine. Use your abdominal muscles to support your body weight as you stand or move.

Did You Know?

80 percent of Americans encounter a lower-back problem sometime in their daily life.

Lifting

Bend your knees, not your back, when lifting. Hold objects close to your body and avoid over-the-head lifts. Avoid rotating your body when lifting or lowering an object. Instead, change your foot placement while maintaining the object directly in front of you.

Sitting at Your Computer Station

Sit in an adjustable chair that keeps your back upright or slightly forward. The adaptable backrest should maintain your body's natural low back curve. Your knees should be slightly lower than your hips. Your feet should be placed solidly on the floor or a footrest. Your keyboard should be at elbow level, with the bend at your elbows near 90 degrees. Your hands and wrists should be straight and relaxed. For some people, wrist rests are preferable. Your eyes should be approximately at a midscreen height of your monitor with your head about an arm's length from the screen.

Sleeping

Try sleeping on your side on a firm mattress with your knees slightly bent or on your back with a pillow under your knees. If you must sleep on your stomach, place a small pillow under your abdominals to correct for a sagging spine.

Did You Know?

The longest and strongest bone in the human body is the femur.

Did You Know?

Nerve cells are the longest cells in the human body.

Back Pain Relief

Back injuries require the attention of a specialist. For relief of small aches, lie on your back on a padded surface and elevate your feet (with bent knees). Place a small pillow or rolled-up towel under your neck and rest in this position for 10 to 15 minutes.

Five Exercises for a Healthy Back

1. **Pelvic Tilt** Lie on your back with knees bent, arms on chest, and feet on floor. Press the lower back into the floor by tightening the abdominal muscles and slightly lifting the buttocks off the floor. Hold for 10 seconds and repeat 8 to 15 times.

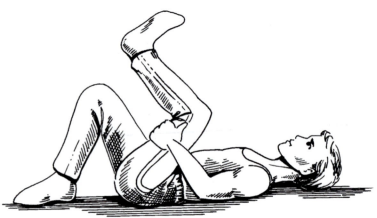

2. **Hamstring Stretch** Lie on your back, with both knees bent and one foot on the floor. Grasp behind the lifted knee, bring it toward the chest, and hold for several seconds. Repeat 3 to 5 times on each leg.

3. **Tuck-Hold** Tuck both knees to chest using your arms to create a tight tuck position. Then, press your lower back into the floor. Keep your back flat. Hold for 15 seconds and repeat 5 to 10 times.

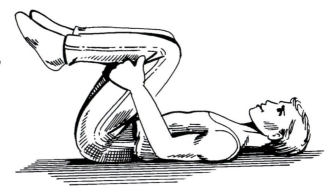

4. **Slow Crunch** Lie on your back with your knees bent at a 45-degree angle and your head supported at the base of the neck by your hands. Slowly lift your chest as you press your lower back into the floor; then slowly lower. Try lifting your buttocks slightly off the floor as you raise the chest. Repeat 8 to 25 times.

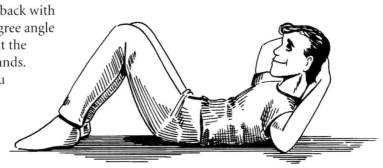

5. **Prone Prop** While on your front, lift your chest off the floor and hold by propping your elbows on the ground. Open your legs slightly.

   Variation: Same as prone prop, only straighten your arms. For both, relax your hips and abdominals and hold for 8 to 15 seconds and then lower. Repeat 3 to 5 times.

Good Posture Promotes Good Health

What is Good Posture and What is Faulty Posture?

The word 'posture' comes from the Latin verb 'ponere' which means to put or place. It refers to the position of the human body in space. Good posture can be defined as a state of skeletal and muscular balance and alignment that protects the supporting structures of the body from progressive abnormality and injury. Whether erect, lying, squatting or stooping, good posture allows the muscles of the body to function most proficiently. With good standing posture the body's joints are in a state of stability with the least amount of physical energy being used to sustain this upright position.

Contrariwise, poor posture, often referred to as faulty posture, is an unsatisfactory link of various skeletal structures of the body. It may produce strain on the supporting body framework structures. With faulty posture there is less efficient balance of the body over its base of support. Therefore, any restriction, imbalance or misalignment of the skeletal structures will have an adverse affect on the movement effectiveness of the person.

Test Your Posture

Test your posture by standing with your hips, back and head against a wall while looking at yourself in a mirror. Place your heels a couple of inches away from the wall. Test for the following:

Head: Not rotated or tilted

Shoulders: Level with no depression or elevation

Lower back: There should be a small space between your lower back and the wall

Pelvis: The hips should be level

Lower extremities: Straight and not bowed

Feet: Facing parallel or with slight out-toeing

Nutrient Timing: A Cutting Edge Training Tip

Exercise enthusiasts regularly seek to improve their strength, stamina, and muscle power through consistent exercise and proper nutrition. In the areas of nutrition and exercise physiology, nutrient timing is 'buzzing' with scientific interest. With appropriate nutrient timing you will be able to more effectively repair muscle tissue damage, restore physiological function, replenish glycogen (stored form of glucose) stores, and promote muscle growth . . . that pretty much says it all.

Nutrient timing is the application of knowing when to eat and what to eat before and after exercise. It is designed to help athletes and exercise enthusiasts achieve their most advantageous exercise performance and recovery. There are two distinct phases in the nutrient timing system.

The Energy Phase: What to Do Before Exercise?

Muscle glycogen is the primary fuel (followed by fat) used by the body during exercise. Low muscle glycogen stores result in muscle fatigue and the body's inability to complete high intensity exercise. Both aerobic and anaerobic exercise decrease glycogen stores, so the need for carbohydrates is high for all types of exercise during this energy phase.

Prior to aerobic exercise, protein intake combined with carbohydrate ingestion has been shown to stimulate protein synthesis post-exercise. This same nutrient combination prior to resistance training can increase the body's capacity to perform more sets, repetitions and prolong a resistance training workout. A combined carbohydrate to protein supplement drink in a 4 to 1 ratio is recommended within 30 minutes of exercise. This will best fuel the energy needs of the body for the workout.

The Anabolic Phase: The 45-Minute Optimal Window After Exercise

The anabolic phase is a critical phase occurring within 45 minutes post-exercise. It is during this time that muscle cells are particularly sensitive. It is also during this time that specialized hormones begin working to repair the muscle, decrease its inflammation and promote muscle growth.

A combined carbohydrate to protein supplement drink in a 3 to 1 or a 4 to 1 ratio will best provide the body with the necessary fuel to initiate the recovery process after exercise. This will increase protein synthesis for cell growth and repair. Interestingly, research has shown that low-fat chocolate milk is an ideal post-workout recovery drink.

SECTION 3

LCC FITNESS CENTERS INFORMATION

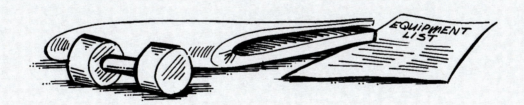

Lansing Community College Fitness Centers

Welcome to the Lansing Community College Fitness Centers
Main and West Campus

▶ What are your Fitness Goals? How many days do you plan to attend, how long will each exercise session be, do you exercise anywhere else, and do you have any injuries or complications?

▶ Work with an instructor to design a program that meets your goals

▶ If you have health concerns, such as joint pain, knee injuries, concerns about cardiovascular health, etc., it is imperative that you contact your health care provider. Some muscular discomfort from lifting or completing a cardiovascular workout should be expected, but this discomfort should be muscle specific and resolved quickly. Chronic pain needs to be evaluated by your health care professional.

Cardiovascular/Aerobic Exercise

▶ Your heart is a muscle and needs to be worked just like skeletal muscles

CARDIOVASCULAR EXERCISE GUIDELINES	
Frequency	3–5x/week
Intensity	• Moderate to vigorous intensity • Target zone • Somewhat hard level (Perceived Exertion) • Talk test
Type (Mode)	jogging, walking, biking, swimming, elliptical machine, stair stepper, Nordic walking, x-country skiing, etc.
Time (Duration)	30–60 minutes—cumulative time—(combined cardio exercises and/or cross training)

Muscular Strength and Endurance Exercise

MUSCULAR STRENGTH AND ENDURANCE EXERCISE GUIDELINES	
Frequency	2–3x/week
Intensity	2–3 sets/10–15 reps at 60–80% 1Rm (Resisteance Maximum)
Type (Mode)	8–10 major muslce groups
Time (Duration)	2–3 sets/10–15 reps 60–80 minutes

General Weight Lifting Techniques

▶ Breathing Techniue while lifting–breathing out on muscle contractions to avoid spikes in blood pressure

▶ Using slow and controlled movements

▶ Proper positioning on the machine

▶ Training opposing muscle groups

▶ Talk to an instructor regarding the design of a program specific to your goals (circuit, split routine, etc.)

Flexibility Exercise

FLEXIBILITY EXERCISE GUIDELINES	
Frequency	2–3x/week ideal 5–7x/week
Intensity	to mild discomfort
Type (Mode)	static and PNF (two person stretch) slow sustained stretching
Time (Duration)	Hold 15–30 seconds repeat 2–4x

SECTION 4
LET'S WORK OUT

The Physiology of Working Out

Energy Systems Provide the Fuel for Exercise

As you embark on some of your many exercises and workouts, it is essential to understand how your body is responding and adapting to these workouts. To exercise and do work for daily life activities, your body uses a chemical compound called ATP (adenosine triphosphate) like a car uses gasoline. ATP is produced by metabolizing (or breaking down) the carbohydrates and fats from the foods you eat. Proteins are used only sparingly for fuel during exercise. Depending on the intensity and duration of the activity, you produce ATP through aerobic and anaerobic metabolism.

Aerobic (which literally means with oxygen) metabolism is the most efficient and main energy production system of the body. This metabolic pathway cannot work unless there is sufficient oxygen available in the tissues during exercise. Prolonged vigorous activity over 5 minutes activates your aerobic metabolism. During prolonged exercises such as cycling, cross-country skiing, and distance running, muscle contraction is dependant on the ability of the aerobic metabolic pathways to continuously regenerate ATP. Mitochondrial respiration (aerobic metabolism in the mitochondrion of the cell) becomes the primary supplier of ATP. Think of the mitochondrion as the 'energy power plant' of your body's cells. As noted previously, fats in the form of triglycerides are available for ATP production, but their breakdown is much slower than glucose and glycogen (which both come from carbohydrates). In fact, decreased levels of blood glucose and low levels of muscle glycogen are associated with the onset of fatigue in sustained aerobic exercise events.

Anaerobic (without oxygen) metabolism is used for situations requiring quick bursts of energy, such as lifting weights, running short races, jumping and throwing. Although anaerobic metabolism is less efficient than the aerobic metabolism, it can quickly generate the ATP needed at the muscle site for needed bursts of energy. Anaerobic metabolism may be called on during aerobic conditioning if the intensity increases beyond the ability of the aerobic system to deliver ATP (such as finishing a long run with a sprint or a section of high kicks during an aerobic program). The two anaerobic metabolic systems are the phosphagen and glycolytic (break down of carbohydrates without the assistance of oxygen) energy system.

During vigorous anaerobic exercise bouts, such as sprinting and high intensity resistance exercise, continued muscle contraction is dependent on the formation of ATP for the demanding exercise. Under these exercise conditions, creatine phosphate, a molecule which resynthesizes ATP and glucose breakdown (called glycolysis) is primarily responsible for maintaining ATP levels. It has been found that during intense muscle contraction, creating phosphate becomes depleted rapidly, resulting in an incomplete supply of ATP. To make-up for this ATP deficiency, glycolysis increases. However, the increased output of glycolysis results in the accumulation of by-products, including lactate and protons (hydrogen ions also shown regularly as H+), which have been identified as potential contributors to fatigue. Historically, researchers have associated lactate (or lactic acid) production during increased rates of glycolysis with the development of cellular acidosis, or what we commonly call 'the burn'. However, more recent research has shown the proton (H+) accumulation is the cause of acidosis in muscle.

The Cardiorespiratory System Delivers the Oxygen

The biochemical reactions involved in mitochondrial respiration depend on continuous oxygen availability for proper functioning. Enhanced oxygen delivery and utilization during exercise will improve mitochondrial respiration and subsequently the capacity for endurance exercise. The oxygen is delivered by the red blood cells to the working muscle and transported into the mitochondrion where it is used in the aerobic production of ATP. There are two major components of the cardiorespiratory system. The heart and lungs, which deliver the oxygen to the working muscle, are called the central component. The ability of exercising muscles to extract and utilize oxygen, which has been transported by the red blood cells, is referred to as the peripheral component. With consistent aerobic training both the central and peripheral component of the cardiorespiratory system improve spectacularly.

The Muscles Are the 'Engines' that Do the Work

Your skeletal muscles attach to the skeleton and contract continuously during exercise. Your bones provide the structure for muscles to attach so that our bodies are able to move. Think of muscles as 'engines' causing the movement of your body and the skeleton as a complex arrangement of levers, fulcrums and force arms that do carry out the movements. The muscles get numerous signals to contract from your nervous system. Muscles are incredibly intricate, with the ability to combine oxygen from the cardiorespiratory system with ATP from the metabolic system for you to do long-lasting exercise. Interestingly, your skeletal muscles work in pairs. One muscle will move a bone in one direction and its paired muscle will move the bone the other way. Your skeletal muscles contract voluntarily, meaning that you think about contracting them and your nervous system tells them to do so.

As you begin these exercises and workouts in *Anybody's Guide to Total Fitness* you will notice that you are breathing heavier and faster during your aerobic workouts. Your sweating is the body's way of dissipating the heat that is generated by your contracting muscles. That is why it is always important to drink water before, during and after exercise. You are encouraged to try many of the different exercises and workouts in the book. Each will use different muscles of your body or the same muscles in different ways. This will enhance the benefits you receive from your exercise participation. Let's get started.

Warm Up First

The purpose of the warm-up is to prepare the body for the more rigorous demands of the cardiorespiratory and/or muscular strength and conditioning segments of the workout.

WARM-UP DO'S AND DON'TS	
Do's	**Don'ts**
Move slowly and rhythmically.	Bounce, jerk or force positions.
Focus on full body range of motion.	"Lock" your joints.
Perform all warm-up exercises on both sides.	

First Off: Active Start

Begin with three to five minutes of **easy** aerobics, brisk walking, or cycling to elevate the body temperature, stimulate circulation to the muscles, and loosen up the joints to prepare them for more strenuous exercise.

   Then, try the following series of warm-up exercises:

Did You Know?

The human body has over 50 trillion cells and that the nerve cells are the longest.

Head
(For neck)

Action: Take head from one side, forward, and around to other side. Reverse. Also, turn head from side to side.

Tips: Avoid taking the head to a straight back position. Make sure these movements are performed slowly.

Shoulder Rolls
(For shoulders)

Action: Smooth circles with shoulders (arms down at side).

Tips: Circle in both directions.

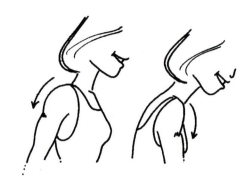

Torso Side Stretch
(For side and hips)

Action: Reach one arm over your head and stretch your torso sideways. Stretch other side. Keep the knees slightly bent.

Tips: Be sure to face forward so you don't twist as you stretch. Support yourself with your extended arm on the thigh to avoid spinal stress.

Torso Twist
(For spine)

Action: Twist gently and rhythmically from the waist.

Tips: Keep your knees slightly bent and control the movement.

Arm Reaches
(For upper back)

Action: Reach with alternating arms over the head, lengthening the upper torso.

Tips: Keep your weight evenly balanced with your lower body. Look up slightly as you do your reaches.

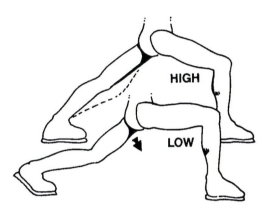

Lunge Stretch: High and Low
(For thighs and lower leg)

Action: Bend front knee and keep back leg straight.
High Lunge: Stretch the Achilles tendon and calf by gently bending and straightening the back leg.
Low Lunge: Stretch the hips down into the floor. Other side.

Tips: Keep the front knee over the ankle and the toes pointing forward.

Upper Spine/Shoulder Stretch

Action: Place hands on thighs above knees. Keep your knees bent. Press one shoulder down and allow the trunk and head to rotate, stretching the upper back, shoulder, and neck. To other side.

Tips: Always keep your knees slightly bent and do not bend over too far forward.

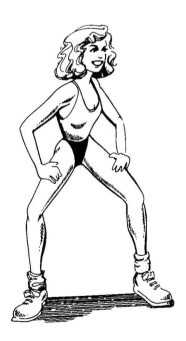

Aerobics: The Main Event

Following are some aerobic steps you can perform to lively music. Start gradually at a brisk walking pace, increase your intensity into your target zone, and then wind back down to a brisk walk. To improve your aerobic efficiency, build up to between 20 and 60 continuous minutes, three to five times a week. Be creative and "choreograph" your own routines! You can create variety by using various arm positions, lifting your legs to different heights, adding a clap, and traveling in a circle or in different directions. Also, all aerobic skills can be modified by just bending and lifting the legs without "bouncing" on the floor. This is called "low-impact" aerobics. A combination of "low-impact" with "impact" aerobics is recommended to reduce the potential of overuse injuries on the body's lower extremities. This is referred to as a "mixed-impact" aerobic workout.

AEROBIC REMINDERS
▶ Wear good aerobic shoes.
▶ Listen to your body.
▶ Check your exercise heart rate to make sure you are in your personalized target zone. As well, periodically monitor your exercise intensity with the perceived exertion scale and talk test.
▶ Gradually increase your exercise intensity.
▶ Make floor contact with your whole foot.
▶ Do not hop on one foot more than four times in a row.
▶ Stay away from twisting hop variations (stress on the spine). Drink water during exercise; your thirst doesn't keep up with your body's need for water.
▶ Important: gradually wind down your aerobics to a brisk walking pace. This is called the aerobic cool-down.

Did You Know?

10 billion white blood cells are made every day.

JOGGING IN PLACE

STEP KNEE HOPS

STEP KICKS

**JUMP
ROPE
HOPS**

**SIDE
LEG
SLIDES**

POWER RUNS

SKI HOPS

JUMPING JACKS

LUNGE CLAPS

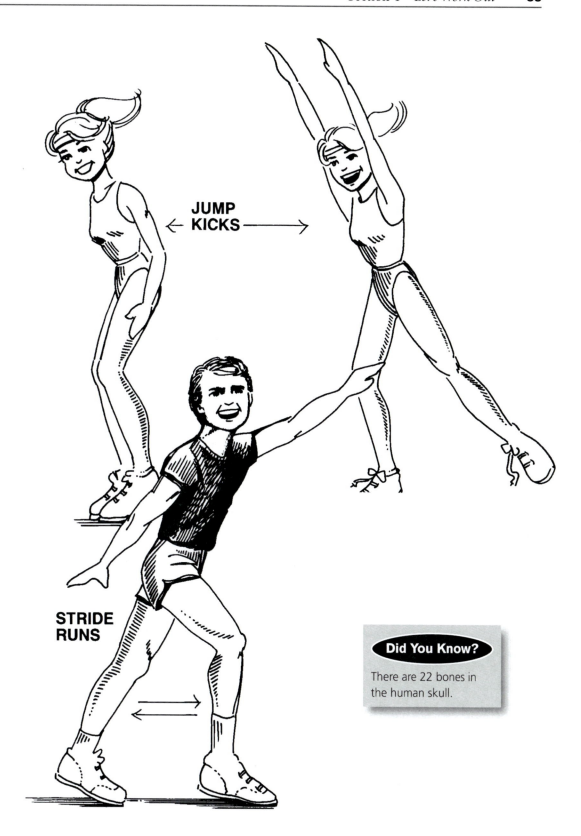

JUMP
KICKS

STRIDE
RUNS

Did You Know?

There are 22 bones in
the human skull.

Stepping Up

Stepping is a very popular group exercise activity. It offers a considerable amount of variety to aerobic exercise classes while contributing to the concept of cross-training. The recognized originator of this famously popular exercise activity discovered it accidentally. While doing knee rehabilitation exercises on a bench, this aerobic professional noted that it could be made much more enjoyable if done to music with a little movement creativity. Fitness professionals and enthusiasts worldwide are the fortunate recipients of this person's inventive contribution to fitness.

Stepping can best be described as a low-impact activity capable of providing high-intensity aerobic conditioning for the participant. The workout can be as challenging as vigorous jogging and yet produce impact forces as safe as walking. The feeling of this activity is very similar to the workout you get from climbing stairs. The cadence of the stepping is slower than the movement tempos you would use in an aerobic class (approximately 118 to 126 beats per minute), because of the greater ranges of motion offered by the platform and because of a concern for safety.

Steps range in height from 4 inches to 12 inches and have a stepping surface of 14 inches wide and up to 4 feet long. It is recommended that you begin gradually, using a lower height step, and progressively increase toward higher step platforms as you become more capable of handling the challenging work. Step workouts are excellent additions to the other aerobic workouts you enjoy doing.

I have presented the basic steps and patterns for you to learn on your step. Treat this workout like any other workout. You need to warm up your body the same as prescribed in the warm-up section. Devote a little more time to warm up the ankles for a step training workout. Accompany this workout with specific body sculpturing exercises of your choice, and don't forget your cooldown stretches at the end of the workout. Each step is most easily categorized by the direction in which the body faces the platform. The specific directions include:

► From the front

► From the side

► From a straddle stand

► From the top

► From the end

Each step is further classified as either a basic or single lead step where the same foot leads every cycle, or as an alternating step where the lead step alternates every four counts. When doing a single lead step, a good rule to follow is to lead with the same leg for no more than 1 minute before changing to the other foot. When doing an alternating lead step, a good rule to follow is to continue the step for no longer than 2 minutes. What about arm choreography? Focus on learning the basic steps at first. Arm choreography will come naturally as you become more comfortable with your stepping patterns.

Here are some basic moves to get you stepping.

Basic Step

a. Directional approach: From the front.

b. Performance: Right foot up, left foot up, right foot down, left foot down, and continue. (Do on both sides.)

c. Pattern: Up, up, down, down.

Alternating Basic Step

a. Directional approach: From the front.

b. Performance: Right foot up, left foot up, right foot down, left foot down (tap), switch lead to left foot up, right foot up, left foot down, right foot down (tap) switch lead, and continue.

c. Pattern: Up, up, down, tap, up, up, down, tap.

Basic V-Step

a. Directional approach: From the front.

b. Performance: Right foot up and out, left foot up and out, right foot down, left foot down, and continue. (Do on both sides.)

Performance Tip: Step with a wide V pattern by opening the legs on top of the platform and bringing them together on the floor.

c. Pattern: Up, up, down, down.

d. Variation: Can also do with an alternating basic step pattern.

Alternating Knee-up Step

a. Directional approach: From the front.

b. Performance: Right foot up, left knee up, left foot down, right foot down. Left foot up, right knee up, right foot down, left foot down. Continue pattern.

c. Pattern: Up, knee, down, down; up other knee, down, down.

Across the Top Step

a. Directional approach: From the side.

b. Performance: Right foot up, left foot up, right foot down, left foot down (tap), switch to left foot up, right foot up, left foot down, right foot down (tap). Continue the alternating across the top pattern.

c. Pattern: Up, across, down, tap; up, across, down, tap.

Straddle Down Step

a. **Directional approach:** From the top.

b. **Performance:** Right foot down on side of platform, left foot down on side of platform, right foot up, left foot up. (Do on both sides.)

c. **Pattern:** Down, down, up, up.

d. **Variation:** Can also do with an alternating step pattern.

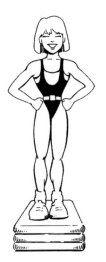

Straddle Up Step

a. **Directional approach:** From a straddle stand.

b. **Performance:** Right foot up, left foot up, right foot down, left foot down. (Do on both sides.)

c. **Pattern:** Up, up, down, down.

d. **Variation:** Can also do with an alternating step pattern.

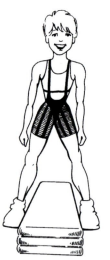

Alternating Straddle Knee Lift Step

a. **Directional approach:** From a straddle stand.

b. **Performance:** Right foot up, left knee lift, left foot down to floor, right foot down to floor. Left foot up, right knee lift, right knee down to floor, left foot down to floor. Continue the alternating knee lift pattern.

c. **Pattern:** Up, knee lift, down, down; Up, knee lift, down, down.

Alternating Side Lunge Step

a. **Directional approach:** From the top.

b. **Performance:** Right foot down and out, right foot on top of platform; left foot down and out, left foot on top of platform. Continue alternating from side to side.

c. **Pattern:** Lunge out, up, lunge out, up.

From the End Step

a. **Directional approach:** From the end.

b. **Performance:** Use the end of the platform to combine several of the steps introduced earlier for variety.

Stepping Safety

1. **Make sure you step entirely on the top part of the platform with each step, not allowing any part of your foot to hang over the edge.**

2. **Start with a 4 inch or 6 inch height.** Don't rush to raise the height of the bench. Most exercisers find the 6 inch height to provide a satisfactory workout. The recommendation to avoid flexing the knee more than 90 degrees with your step height is a conservative guideline that is easy to follow.

3. **Adding handheld weights (up to 4 lbs.) changes your arm choreography to slow, controlled, nonrotational, shorter-lever movements.**

4. **Stop stepping and march in place on the ground whenever you want to lower the intensity.**

5. **Be careful not to step too far back off the platform.** This causes the body to lean slightly forward, placing extra stress on the Achilles tendon and calf.

6. **Use a good cross-training shoe or indoor fitness shoe for your workout.** The tread on some running shoes does not provide suitable freedom of movement or support.

7. **Step onto and off the platform.** Avoid pounding your feet on the ground and platform. Also, try not to step with a bounce; this causes you to remain on the balls of your feet.

8. **Remember not to lock your knees on the descending phase of the step pattern.**

9. **Avoid any movements that travel forward and down off the bench.**

10. **Drink plenty of water, as you tend to sweat a little more with step training.**

11. **Be aware of the potential for overuse injury syndrome.** Many people will enjoy the variety and uniqueness of step training so much that they will discontinue their other physical activities. Doing a variety of exercise programs lessens the stress on many specific body parts, and still allows you to place a lot of demands on your body.

12. **If you feel any discomfort underneath or around the knee you need to stop.** See your health practitioner. Bench stepping may not be the best activity for you.

13. **Always watch your platform when stepping, but don't drop the head forward.** Also, move your arms through low, mid, and high ranges of motion.

14. **As you step, avoid unnecessary forward bending at the hips.** This may put too much stress on your back.

15. **Be careful of overusing the lunge skills.** They can cause you to lean too far forward, stressing your lower back, and they can place extra joint trauma on the lower leg with ground impact.

16. **Change the leading foot of your stepping patterns regularly to avoid over-stressing one leg.** A good rule of thumb is to not lead with one leg for more than a minute.

17. **To avoid stress on the leg, do not perform more than five consecutive repeating movements on the same leg.**

Aerobic Kickboxing: A Knockout Punch

Aerobic kickboxing, kickbox fitness, box-step and cardio-karate are a few class names that have become a staple core of the group-led exercise industry. Enthusiasts are enjoying the power from throwing kicks, punches, elbows, jabs, knee strikes, and combinations used in boxing and kickboxing. The athletic drills in these classes are mixed with recovery bouts of basic aerobic movements such as boxer-style rope skipping and easy jogging. Some programs utilize authentic boxing and martial arts equipment whereas others do a form of "shadow boxing." All classes are driven by high-energy music and have provided a new alternative to group-led exercise classes, which appeal to both women and men. Research by this author suggests that the energy cost of this type of exercise ranges from 6.5 to 8.4 kilocalories a minute for a 130-pound female.

With the popularity and excitement however, some new challenges have surfaced such as safety for the participants. A key concern is that instructors have the proper knowledge to teach correct punching techniques. The challenge involves integrating skill with a motivating workout environment. Several organizations have established their own standards of safety, but there are no nationally accepted guidelines among certifying groups. The best advice to participants is to make sure the class instructor has had some type of specialized training and/or certification. Instructors need to be aware of the appropriate development skills and precautions to use when teaching these martial arts workouts.

Aerobic Kickboxing Safety Guidelines

1. With all upper body jabs and strikes, keep your elbows from locking out.

2. Avoid performing complex upper body strike and lower body kick combinations.

3. Avoid high repetitions of any aerobic kickboxing move.

4. Do not do physical contact exercises without proper skill progressions.

5. Kicking and pivoting may lead to lower extremity injury. Always master the basic moves before progressing to advanced kickboxing movements.

6. Safe music speeds for aerobic kickboxing are from 120 to 135 bpm.

7. Be aware that the newness of kickboxing movements may lead to more delayed-onset muscle soreness when starting this type of program.

8. Give yourself plenty of floor space with doing your kickboxing movements.

9. Deliver punches from the body as opposed to from the shoulders.

Aquatic Exercise Workouts

Water fitness classes (in 81° to 84°) are steadily growing in popularity with all fitness levels. These workouts have been shown to postively reduce percent body fat and improve muscular fitness. The three water depths used in water fitness classes are (1) shallow, which is navel to nipple; (2) transitional, which is nipple to neck; and (3) deep, where the feet are not touching the bottom. Lower body exercises in shallow water level incorporate more jumping and leaping exercise movements. In deep water exercise, where some type of buoyancy is used, the lower body challenge can be intensified with the use of aquatic exercise equipment to add more resistance to the movement. Always reduce the speed of the exercises in water as compared to similar movements on land. In fact, it is often preferable to self-adjust your exercise movement speed in water based on your own level of perceived exertion. Also, several types of aquatic equipment (such as fins, webbed gloves, and nonbuoyant bells) have been designed to provide a variety of different exercise options in aquatic exercise workouts. In aquatic exercise, attempt to keep your entire body in motion during the entire water workout. Try to always combine upper and lower body exercises and enjoy the variety of this wonderful workout.

Did You Know?

A human neck has the same number of vertebra as a giraffe.

Indoor Cycling Workouts

Indoor cycling classes are very popular aerobic workouts. Because of its non-weight bearing nature, indoor cycling workouts offer some orthopedic advantages for anyone having limitations with weight-bearing exercise. With indoor cycling, it is common to visualize you are on a 'virtual' outdoor race or scenic ride (with hills, curves, straight-aways, and valleys), where you pace your exercise intensity according to the demands of the situation. Motivational music and softer room lighting really enhance this type of aerobic work-out. Because of the stationary nature of this workout, adequate air circulation is quite important. You can adjust your inten-sity with your wheel resistance, ped-aling speed and body position (seated or standing) while cycling. Make sure you are fitted correctly for your bike. Your downstroking knee should never lock out when extended and your upstroking knee should not exceed the level of your hip. Always wear cycling shorts with padded inserts to lesson any discom-fort from the prolonged sitting. A hard-soled cycling shoe is rec-ommended to decrease pressure on the feet while pedaling. Make sure your

shoes provide plenty of movement space in the toe area to avoid numbness in the ball of the foot. Also, make sure you are fully aware of the operation and adjustments of the exercise bike before starting. Don't forget to bring your water bottle with you and a towel to wipe off your seat as you exercise. It is a heathful idea to vary your riding position during the workout to lessen the stress on your lower back. As well, don't place too much body weight on the handlebars during the standing position cycling. As these classes are sometimes quite strenuous, plan for a longer and more grad-ual cooldown when finishing this highly enjoyable workout.

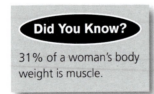

Did You Know?

31% of a woman's body weight is muscle.

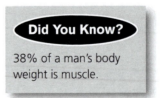

Did You Know?

38% of a man's body weight is muscle.

Are You Ready for a High Intensity Interval Training Workout?

The fitness industry is experiencing a rise in popularity of high intensity interval training, often referred to as HIIT workouts. This system of training involves repeated bouts of high intensity efforts followed by recovery periods of varying lengths of time. HIIT actually dates back to the early 1900's. Many studies demonstrate that HIIT can increase the performance benefits of competitive athletes and improve the health of recreational exercisers. Plus, you can do HIIT training on any mode of exercise you like such as walking, treadmill running, cycling, stair climbing and elliptical training.

HIIT Program Development

When developing a HIIT program the duration, intensity, and frequency of the work intervals is always considered along with the length of the recovery intervals. Intensity during the high intensity work bout should range ≥ 80% of your personalized target zone (see The Formula for Aerobic Fitness on page 22). The intensity of the recovery interval should be 50–70% of your personalized target zone.

The relationship of the work and recovery interval is also a consideration. Many studies use a specific ratio of exercise to recovery to improve the different energy systems of the body. For example, a ratio of 1:1 might be a 3-minute hard work (or high intensity) bout followed by a 3-minute recovery (or low intensity) bout, which is what I have designed for *Anybody's Guide to Total Fitness* readers.

Follow these steps to do your HIIT workout.

1. IMPORTANTLY, always do a good warm-up before and an appropriate cool-down after your HIIT workout.

2. Determine what mode of exercise you wish to complete your HIIT workout. For instance, you can do this on cycling, elliptical training, walking indoors and outdoors, treadmill running, stair climbing, rowing and all other modes of exercise.

3. Let's use the 1:I ratio with a 3-minute high intensity bout followed by a 3-minute recovery bout.

4. Determine your 80% personalized target zone for your high intensity bouts. Note, you can always work at a harder intensity but let's start with this intensity. This would be a 16 or 'Hard' on the Perceived Exertion Scale.

5. Determine your 60% personalized target zone for your recovery bouts. This can be between 50% and 70%, so let's stay right in the middle of that range. This would be an 11 or 'Fairly light' on the Perceived Exertion Scale.

6. Each interval is comprised of a 3-minute high intensity bout followed by a 3-minute recovery bout. To stay within ACSM duration guidelines for cardiorespiratory endurance (see page 186) let's do 4 intervals (high intensity bout followed by a recovery bout, into by a 2nd high intensity bout and recovery bout, into a 3rd high intensity bout and recovery bout into the 4th high intensity bout and recovery bout, followed by your cooldown). This HIIT workout will be 24 minutes plus your warm-up and cool-down.

Did You Know?

The majority of energy producing chemical reactions in the body occur in the mitochondrion.

7. Use a watch to time your intervals and a heart rate monitor to monitor your heart rate during the workout.

8. Here are a couple of HIIT tips. Do not do more than 3 HIIT workouts a week to allow your body to fully recover and to prevent overtraining. Try doing HIIT on different modes of exercise.

Did You Know?

A hiccup is your diaphragm contracting rapidly.

Body Conditioning Workouts

Four different body conditioning programs follow for your training variety. They are:

1. Site-specific exercise section for distinctive body areas.

2. Super sculpturing program with hand weights.

3. Circuit training course with complete instructions on how to progressively overload the program.

4. Power sculpturing exercises and workout.

For best body shaping results, regularly vary your selection of these workouts to constantly challenge your muscles.

Chest, Shoulder, and Arm Developers

Perform 10 to 30 repetitions of each exercise.

Modified or Regular Push-ups
(Chest, shoulders, and arms)

Action: Lower torso all the way to the floor and up.

Tips: Keep the back straight.

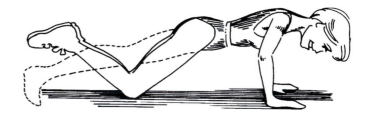

Wide-Arm Push-ups
(Chest and arms)

Action: Same as push-up with arms placed beyond shoulder width. Open legs to a straddle position.

Tips: Make sure fingers are pointed away from body.

Pike Push-ups
(Shoulders and triceps—back of the arms)

Action: A push-up with hips up and hands closer to feet. Legs together or open to a straddle.

Tips: Placing the hands closer together is more challenging.

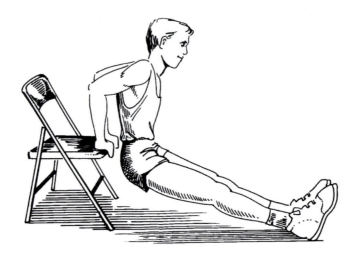

Dips
(Shoulders, chest, and triceps)

Action: With hands by side on chair or floor, bend and extend arms.

Tips: Hands should face forward. Keep legs extended when using chair.

For a Stable Core: The Excellent Eight

Perform 15 to 40 repetitions of each exercise.

Regular Crunch
(Abdominals)

Action: Lift the back and shoulders off the floor. Push the small of the back against the floor. Rotate pelvis so buttocks are slightly off floor.

Tips: Feet are on the floor approximately six to ten inches from the buttocks. Hands may support the head at the base of the neck or lie across the chest. Focus on the ceiling.

Variation: Squeeze your knees together for inner thigh work as well.

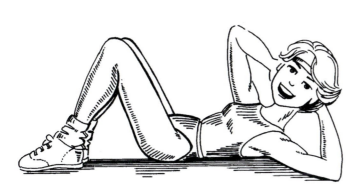

Twisting Crunch
(Abdominals and obliques—sides)

Action: Alternate shoulders as you lift your upper back off the floor.

Tips: Vary your technique by either lifting first and then twisting or by twisting first and then lifting.

Reverse Crunch
(Lower abdominals)

Action: Slowly lift buttocks off the ground a couple of inches.

Tips: Keep the knees bent.

Variation: Bring chest toward knee (as you lift the buttocks) for an even more challenging crunch. Press the heels into the buttocks to relax your hip flexors and work the abdominals more.

Rope Pull Crunch
(Abdominals and obliques)

Action: Lift shoulder blades off the floor and alternate reaching the arms
(as if pulling a rope).

Tips: Make sure the small of the back is pressed
into floor.

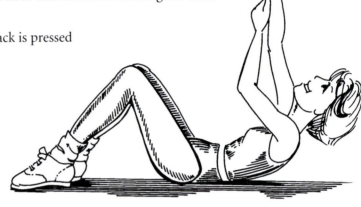

The All-Around Crunch
(Abdominals and obliques)

Action: Alternate with a twisting crunch to
one side, a regular crunch straight up, and a
twisting crunch to the other side.

Tips: Lift the legs so the thighs are perpendicular to the floor and bent at the knees. You
may wish to place your feet on a chair.

Variation: Randomly mix the pattern of the
side, up, other side to surprise your
abdominal muscles—they have to work
harder!

Back Extension
(After working the abdominal muscles,
it is correct to work the opposite muscle group: the lower back.)

Action: Slowly lift the head, shoulders, and chest off the floor from the prone
position. The arms may help with the lift, remain at the
sides, or be held close to the
shoulders.

Tips: Keep the feet on the
floor to protect the spine.
Stretch up and out.

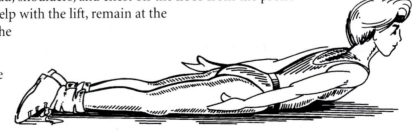

Horizontal Side Bridge
(Deep abdominals and spinal muscles)

Action: Do this exercise on a padded surface. Lie on your side with the knees bent at about a 90-degree angle. With the abdominals pulled in, push up with the elbow, lifting the torso off the ground. Hold for 6 to 12 seconds and then lower and repeat several times on both sides.

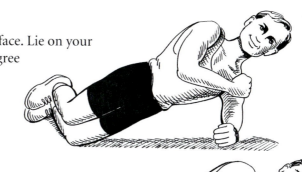

Tips: Keep the nonsupportive hand on the opposite shoulder.

Variation: For greater challenge, do the exercise with the knees off the floor and legs extended.

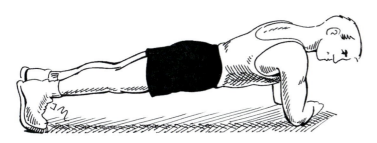

Rolling Side Bridge
(Deep abdominals and spinal muscles)

Action: Lie on your side with your legs extended. Pull in the abdominal muscles and push up to a side bridge. Roll slowly to a front prone position with both elbows on the ground and then roll to the other elbow.

Tips: Move very slowly and work up to repeating this entire sequence for up to 30 to 45 seconds or until the muscles fatigue.

Variation: For a more challenging side bridge, place the upper foot in front of the lower foot. This will cause more instability, making you work your intrinsic spinal muscles even more.

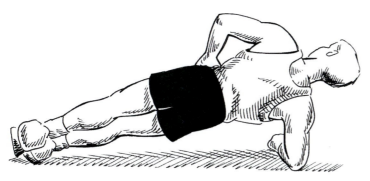

Thighs, Hips, and Buttocks

These body parts are best worked together! Use elastic resistance or exercise equipment or wear leg weights for an adequate overload. Perform 15 to 30 repetitions of each exercise.

Back Thigh Lifts
(Back thigh, buttocks, and hip)

Action: Keeping an erect standing position with the resistance on one ankle, bring the leg toward the rear to a comfortable ending point.

Tips: For balance, place one arm on an immobile surface.

Variation: Do this exercise slightly toward the angle (between straight back and to the side). It works the same muscles and some people find it more comfortable.

Hip Adduction
(Inner thigh)

Action: From a standing position, extend one leg to the side making sure you feel a moderate resistance on the leg. Pull the leg in front and across the midline of the body. Return slowly to starting position.

Tips: Try not to let the body twist during this exercise.

Variation: Hold leg across midline of movement for 3 seconds before returning to starting position.

Hip Abduction
(Outer thighs and hips)

Action: From a standing position with feet together and resistance strap around the outer leg, lift the leg straight to the side.

Tips: Do not let the body swing from side to side and keep your feet facing forward.

Variation: Hold the movement for 3 seconds out to the side before returning to starting position.

Bird-Dog Exercise
(Buttocks and lower back)

Action: Starting on the hands and knees, slowly raise one arm and the opposite leg to a horizontal position and hold for 6 seconds. Lower the arm and leg and then repeat with the other arm and opposite leg. Repeat several times.

Tips: Pull in the abdominals while doing this exercise.

Variation: You can also do this exercise while lying in a prone position.

Tightening Tips

▶ Remember to repeat all exercises on both sides. Vary your exercise performance tempo.

▶ There is a tendency in leg work to roll back at the hip and let the powerful quadriceps (front of the thigh muscles) do the work—watch your technique.

▶ It is not necessary to lift the legs high for results.

▶ Combine full range-of-motion exercises with "pulse" movements—take the leg to the top end of the range and perform small "pulse" movements.

Inner Thigh Extras

Inner Thigh Lifts—Knee Down

Action: Lie on side with head supported by bent arm or resting on straight arm. Bring top leg over extended bottom leg and relax top knee into the floor. Lift lower leg up and down.

Tips: Concentrate on lifting with bottom heel. Perform 15 to 30 repetitions. You may need to use ankle weights to effectively challenge your inner thighs.

Inner Thigh Lifts—Knee Up

Action: Same as above. Place top leg over bottom leg with foot in front of knee. Lift lower leg up and down.

Tips: Concentrate on lifting with bottom heel. Perform 15 to 30 repetitions.

Wide Squats

Action: Stand with feet placed wider than shoulders. Keeping your back straight, bend your knees until your buttocks are slightly above knee height. Hold this position for 15 to 30 seconds.

Tips: Make sure your knees point directly over your toes.

Variation: While in this squat position go up and down very slowly and focus on using the muscles of the inner thigh.

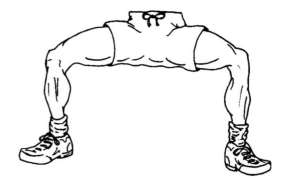

Super Sculpturing with Weights

If you really want to attain that sleek, firm, and shapely look, use weights. You can work all the major muscles of the body with hand weights. Perform 8 to 20 repetitions of each exercise, doing two to four sets of each exercise. Be sure to rest 30 to 60 seconds between sets.

Squat
(Buttocks and thighs)

Action: Stand with feet placed wider than shoulders. Hold weights into chest or next to shoulders. Keeping your back straight, bend legs and squat down with your buttocks no lower than your knee height and return to start.

Tips: Make sure your buttocks go back as you sit and your knees stay over your toes. Do this carefully if you have knee problems!

Variation: Change the width of your stance to work all the muscles completely.

Long Lunge
(Thighs and buttocks)

Action: Stand with feet together and hand weights next to shoulder or down by your side. Step forward about two to three feet with one leg to a bent knee position. Keep the back leg extended, allowing it to bend slightly. Push back to a stand and repeat on other leg.

Tips: Keep your back straight and press into the bending leg.

Variation: Stand with feet together and hand weights by side. "Step back" into lunge position.

Short Lunge
(Thighs and buttocks)

Action: Stand with one foot two to three feet in front of the other foot. Hold weights next to your sides. Bend both legs so the back knee comes within six inches of the ground and then straighten up. Do on both sides.

Tips: Turn toes out slightly for balance.

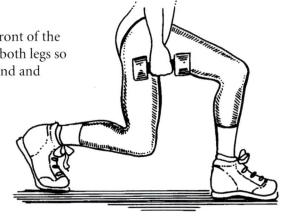

Heel Raises
(Calves)

Action: Stand with legs wider than shoulder width, feet slightly turned out. Hold weights along sides. Lift heels high off the ground and then lower.

Tips: Perform this exercise on a thick book or block of wood to allow a larger range of motion.

Chest Press
(Chest, shoulders, and arms)

Action: Lie on a bench or floor with hand weights held by shoulders. Extend arms straight up and back down to side.

Tips: Keep elbows out from body at the start for effective chest overload. Bend knees with feet on the bench (ground) or with knees pulled toward the chest to safeguard the lower back.

Flys
(Chest and arms)

Action: Same position (on bench or floor) as chest press. Start with hand weights extended above chest and lower arms perpendicularly away from body and then back up.

Tips: Keep arms slightly bent throughout the exercise and palms facing each other.

Variation: Modify the position of the hand weights as they extend over the chest.

Crunches with Weights
(Abdominals)

Action: With back on the floor, weight(s) held behind the head or on the chest, lift upper back off the floor and lower. Lower legs placed on a chair.

Tips: Press the small of the back into the floor.

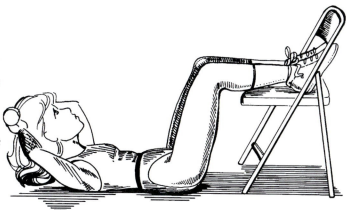

Variation: Twist side to side in the crunch.

Standing Rows
(Upper and middle back)

Action: Stand in a straddle position with head up, upper body slightly forward, and legs partially bent. Hand weights are extended in front of body. Pull elbows as far back as they will go and return to start.

Tips: Do not bend forward too much (this may stress the spine).

Variation: Stand in lunge position with weight in one hand. Bend over at waist and place other hand on bent knee for support. Pull arm straight back and lower.

Shoulder Press
(Shoulders and triceps)

Action: May be done standing or sitting.

Shoulder: Start with hand weights held next to shoulder. Press weights straight over head and return to start.

Tips: Make sure you keep your back stable during the exercise.

Variation: Alternate pressing one arm and then the other arm to concentrate on each side.

Side Lateral Raises
(Shoulders and back)

Action: Hold hand weights next to your side. Keeping arms slightly bent, elevate weights laterally to shoulder height and lower.

Tips: Do not "lock" elbow joints or raise arms above shoulders.

Variation: For more upper back work, sit in a chair and bend forward at hips. Lift weights to shoulder height with bent arms and lower.

Tricep Extensions
(Triceps—back of arms)

Action: Stand with legs shoulder-width apart and knees bent. Bring weights up, bending elbows up and back. From this position, extend arms straight back and then return to start.

Tips: Keep the elbows from swinging forward and back.

Variation: Extend elbows to the side and open arms to the side (no higher than shoulders).

Bicep Curls
(Biceps—front of arms)

Action: Stand with legs shoulder-width apart and knees bent. Bring weights to shoulder and lower.

Tips: Keep the hands in a "palm-up" position.

Variation: Alternate lifting one arm and then the other. Or do the curls in a lunge position.

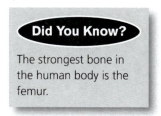

Did You Know?

The strongest bone in the human body is the femur.

Super Sculpture Tips

▶ Find a hand weight that's comfortable, yet challenging.

▶ For variety, vary the number of repetitions, the sequence of exercises, the number of sets, or the weight.

▶ For best results perform this routine two or (preferably) three times a week.

▶ As the weight gets easy to work with, gradually overload with a heavier weight, more repetitions, more sets, or less time between sets.

▶ Try a circuit training format (time effective and good for muscular endurance training): perform a set of each exercise and then move to the next exercise without resting. Perform two to four circuits.

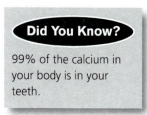

Did You Know?

99% of the calcium in your body is in your teeth.

▶ Refer to *A Circuit Workout* for more on circuit training.

Did You Know?

The longest nerve in the body is the sciatic nerve.

A Circuit Workout

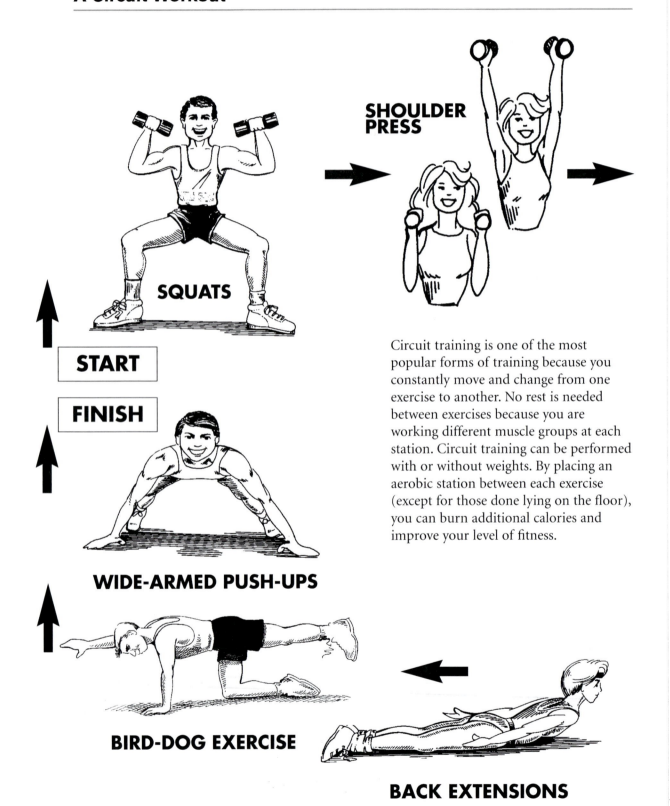

SHOULDER PRESS

SQUATS

START

FINISH

WIDE-ARMED PUSH-UPS

BIRD-DOG EXERCISE

BACK EXTENSIONS

Circuit training is one of the most popular forms of training because you constantly move and change from one exercise to another. No rest is needed between exercises because you are working different muscle groups at each station. Circuit training can be performed with or without weights. By placing an aerobic station between each exercise (except for those done lying on the floor), you can burn additional calories and improve your level of fitness.

POWER LUNGES

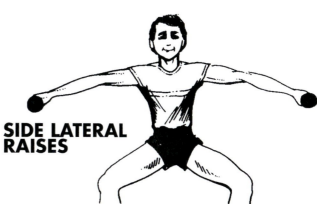

SIDE LATERAL RAISES

Perform 15 to 30 repetitions at each station for a 45-second work interval. Then move to the next station. Go through the circuit two to three times. Try working out to music. Make sure you warm up before you start and stretch out when you finish. You can progressively overload by the following means (but choose only one method at a time):

1. Increase the number of stations.
2. Repeat the circuit another time.
3. Increase the number of repetitions at each station.
4. Increase the load of weights.
5. Increase the pace of the workload.

STANDING ROWS

CRUNCHES   **TRICEP EXTENSIONS**   **BICEP CURLS**

NEW Circuit Study Provides New Training Idea!

A recent study on circuit training offers a unique circuit protocol you may wish to try in the weight room. In this study, the subjects, who were familiar with resistance exercise, completed the following standard weight room exercises in this sequence: leg press, bench press, leg curl, latissimus pull-down, biceps curl, seated shoulder press, triceps push-down, upright row, leg extension and seated row. The subjects completed five circuits of this 10-exercise protocol for the study. However, the subjects performed all of the exercises at 40 percent of their maximum capacity, which means the loads on each exercise were light. For each exercise, the subjects performed 10 repetitions and then moved rapidly to the next station. All repetitions were performed at an even, but slightly brisker tempo (about one second up and one second down on the upward and downward movement phases of each exercise), and the subjects rested no longer than 5 seconds between each exercise—about as long as it took to move to the next exercise and get properly situated to perform the exercise. Not only was this a meaningful muscular endurance workout for the subjects, but also during the workout the subjects managed to maintain a cardiovascular intensity that kept them in their personalized training zone. This unique approach to circuit training provides evidence that muscular endurance and aerobic capacity can be adequately challenged with this training format. Try it and see how you like it—start with 2 circuits and gradually add a circuit (up to 5) as you feel the desire to do more.

Functional Power Exercises

The following functional "power" exercises are original movement combinations biomechanically designed to effectively challenge the body. This program will offer creativity while improving your functional strength and core stability. Begin with a comfortable starting weight and gradually overload with heavier resistance. For variety, perform the standing power exercises in random order, changing movements after every eight repetitions. Do all movements with control.

Power Side
(Abductors, adductors, gluteals, quadriceps, hamstrings, deltoids, triceps)

Action: From a wide squat, extend legs lifting one leg off the ground as you straighten your arms. Return to squat and alternate sides.

Tips: Keep the lifting leg from rotating outward to effectively work the abductors. On all squats, be sure to keep the buttocks at or above standing knee height.

Power Ski
(Abductors, adductors, gluteals, quadriceps, hamstrings, deltoids, pectorals)

Action: From a wide squat, extend legs to lift and flex one leg as you squeeze your elbows together. Return to wide squat and alternate sides.

Tips: Make sure you lift your knee to the side. Keep legs slightly wider than shoulder width in all wide squats.

Power Knee
(Quadriceps, gluteals, hip flexors, deltoids, triceps)

Action: From a narrow squat position with legs close together, extend legs, lifting one leg with a bent knee as you extend the arms over the head. Lower to narrow squat and alternate sides.

Tips: Keep your back straight and the buttocks back as you sit in a narrow squat. Do not go as low in the narrow squat as you do in the wide squat.

Power Deltoid

(Adductors, quadriceps, gluteals, hamstrings, deltoids)

Action: Extend your legs from a squat as you laterally raise your arms to shoulder height. Lower and repeat.

Tips: Raise and lower your arms (with control) making sure to keep them shoulder height or below in the top position.

Power Row

(Spinal extensors, quadriceps, gluteals, hamstrings, trapezius)

Action: Extend your body and legs from a flexed squat position as you lift your elbows above your head.

Tips: Keep your hands close together, stopping them under your chin at the top position. To effectively work the spinal extensors, you need to find a comfortable yet challenging starting position where the trunk is flexed. Keep the head up and the back straight.

Power Lunge
(Quadriceps, hamstrings, gluteals, biceps)

Action: From a standing position with arms by your side, step back into a lunge position and perform a bicep curl with your arms. Return to the starting position and repeat on other side.

Tips: Be sure to keep your bent knee over your ankle and your weight forward.

Variations: Turn your knuckles toward your shoulders and perform a reverse arm curl. You can also vary the degree of difficulty by keeping your knees slightly bent throughout the exercise.

Power Hamstring
(Hamstrings)

Action: Stand with one leg one and a half to two feet in front of the other leg with the toes facing forward. Hold weights down by sides. With your weight supported over your front leg, bend the back leg bringing the heel toward the buttocks and then lower the leg to the floor. Complete repetitions on one leg before switching sides. As the back leg bends, bring the arms up along the torso.

Tips: Do not allow the knee of the working leg to come forward. As you curl the leg, keep the upper body stable to support the lower back.

Power Hip
(Gluteals, hamstrings, triceps)

Action: Stand with one leg one and a half to two feet behind the other leg and slightly out to the side. Bring the weights just under the shoulders. Lift the back leg toward the diagonal plane. Lower leg slowly to floor. As the leg goes back diagonally, the arms extend out to the side and return as the leg lowers to floor. Complete repetitions on one leg before switching sides.

Tips: Squeeze the buttocks as you lift and lower the leg. Try to do the action with a smooth rhythm throughout the range.

Did You Know?

In most adults the spinal cord is about 17 inches long.

Functional Power Workout

The following is a recommended sequence of exercises for a muscular endurance workout. You will effectively work your body's muscular system, progressing from larger (more energy demanding) muscle groups to smaller (more specific) muscles. To overload, vary the number of repetitions, the number of sets, the movement tempo, or the weight. Perform exercises half-time using music with 140 to 150 beats per minute.

- ▶ **Standing Power Moves:** Power side, power ski, power knee, power row, power deltoid, power lunge, power hamstring, power hip

- ▶ **Gastrocnemius/Anterior Tibialis:** Heel raises with feet facing out, forward, and in; toe lifts for anterior tibialis

- ▶ **Pectorals:** Standing flys with bent arms (arms high and low), chest/elbow squeezes

- ▶ **Rhomboids/Trapezius:** Standing row, single arm row, reverse fly (standing or with one knee on the floor)

- ▶ **Abdominals:** Crunch, twisting crunch, rope pull crunch, all-around crunch, reverse crunch (all abdominal exercises with or without hand weights)

- ▶ **Specific Gluteals, Abductors, Adductors:** Prone leg lifts, outer leg lifts, inner thigh lifts

- ▶ **Deltoids:** Shoulder press (in seated position)

- ▶ **Triceps/Deltoid/Chest:** Wide-arm push-ups, pike push-ups, triceps extension on knees (or seated)

- ▶ **Biceps:** Bicep curls and alternating arm bicep curls

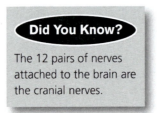

Did You Know?

The 12 pairs of nerves attached to the brain are the cranial nerves.

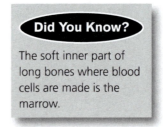

Did You Know?

The soft inner part of long bones where blood cells are made is the marrow.

Stability Ball Training for the 'Core'

Originating in Europe, stability ball training is quite popular throughout the United States. Although originally used in rehabilitation, stability ball training is now used in group-led exercise classes and by home fitness buffs. These round, beach-ball-looking devices provide an unstable base for exercises to be performed. The unstable nature of the ball allows more muscles to be challenged when performing exercises on or with the stability ball. Ball size varies; however, a good rule of thumb when selecting a ball is that when the individual is seated on the ball, her/his hips should be level with the knees. The firmness of the ball is another element to consider. A softer ball has a larger base or surface area, making it easier for the client to maintain balance. Firmer balls definitely provide more balance challenges. With specialized training, you can learn numerous exercises with stability balls. Because 80 percent of Americans suffer from a degree of low-back pain, the exercises shown with the stability ball have been chosen to strengthen the trunk and core musculature. The core muscles stabilize the spine and run the entire length of the torso. Do 8 to 16 repetitions of each exercise.

Supine Trunk Curl
(Rectus abdominous, internal and external obliques)

Starting Position: Supine incline position with arms crossed over the chest or hands placed at the side of the head.

Action: Slowly curl your trunk, letting your shoulders and upper back lift off the ball. Return to starting position and repeat.

Tips: Support your head if your neck becomes fatigued. Think of bringing your ribs to your hips.

Variation: Change your feet position to vary the challenge of balance. The closer the feet are together, the more difficult it is to balance. Also, vary the position of your arms from across the chest, by the side of the head, or extended above the head.

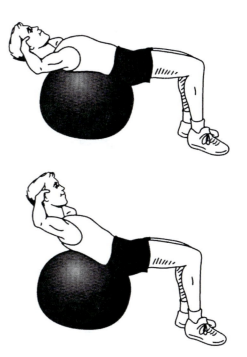

Supine Oblique Rotation
(Rectus abdominous, internal and external
obliques)

Starting position: Supine incline position with arms
crossed over the chest or hands placed at the side of
the head.

Action: Begin by bringing your ribs to the hips. As
you curl your trunk, rotate one side of the upper body
toward the other side. Return to starting position and
repeat, rotating to the other side.

Tips: Always start each exercise with the trunk curl
first. Press the lower back into the ball as you do the
exercise.

Variation: Change your feet position to vary the challenge of balance. The closer the feet are together, the
more difficult to balance. Also, vary the position of your
arms from across the chest, by the side of the head, or
extended to the side of your torso.

Prone Trunk Extension
(Erector spinae, gluteus maximus)

Starting Position: Start prone with your
trunk on the ball. Place your hands to the
side of your head, by your side, or wrapped
around the ball. Allow your trunk to round
over the ball. Spread your legs and keep both
feet solid on the floor.

Action: Slowly extend the spine, lifting your
chest slightly off the ball until the spine is
straight. Return to starting position and
repeat.

Tips: Keep your neck in a neutral position.
Do not overextend your spine.

Variation: Regularly change your arms from
by your side, next to your head, or extended
over your head.

Side-Lying Lateral Flexion
(Internal and external obliques, erector spinae, quadratus lumborum)

Starting Position: Start in a side-lying position on the ball with the bent leg firmly planted on the floor. Place one hand on the ball and bend the arm on the ball, placing the hand on the side of the head. Allow the trunk to round over the ball.

Action: Laterally lift the trunk slowly. Once you reach the top of the motion, return slowly to the starting position and repeat.

Tips: Do not allow your hips to roll forward or backward. Keep your head in its neutral position, not allowing it to dip down, forward, or backward.

Variation: As you get stronger, put both hands to the side of the head with your elbows to the side.

Did You Know?

The left side of your brain is a control center for logic and speech.

Did You Know?

Nerve impulses can travel 250 miles per hour.

START HERE

POWER KNEE

**Power Runs
45–60 seconds**

POWER SIDE

**Side Leg
Slides
45–60
seconds**

Boot Camp Workouts are Happening!

Boot camp workouts are time efficient workouts that challenge your entire body by moving rapidly from one exercise to another with no rest. Initially they were completed outdoors. Now, because of their popularity they are also done regularly indoors and outdoors. They are similar to circuit training workouts which move the exercisers from station to station. The workouts can have a number of movement themes including muscular strength, agility, speed, muscular endurance, power and

**POWER
HAMSTRING**

**Jump Kicks
45–60 seconds**

POWER LUNGE

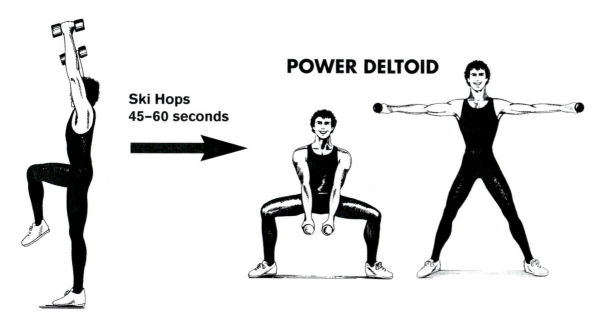

**Ski Hops
45–60 seconds**

POWER DELTOID

aerobic capacity. They also can be designed for different groups including children, seniors, weight loss, women-only, men-only, and sport specific (i.e., cycling, rowing, skiing, etc.). The underlying theme with a boot camp workout is to challenge yourself continuously during the workout, to resemble what occurs in a real military boot camp. For *Anybody's Guide to Total Fitness,* I have incorporated several power exercises (using dumbbells that are described on pages 97–101) that alternate with spirited aerobic exercise moves into a challenging boot camp workout for you to try. Do each exercise for 45–60 seconds and then do the aerobic move for the same length of time before moving to the next exercise. Repeat the boot camp 2–3 times. For safety, please put the dumbbells on the ground when you do your aerobic exercises. Make sure you begin with a thorough warm-up and finish with a cool-down after the boot camp workout. Take yourself to the limit.

**Jump Rope
Hops
45–60
seconds**

**Lunge Claps
45–60 seconds**

POWER ROW

Barefoot Running Program: Have You Tried It Yet?

For many people, running provides a feeling of wellbeing. Many enthusiasts experience feelings of euphoria and stress relief after a good run. Despite its popularity, the incidence of running injuries is relatively high. The majority of running injuries are at the knee, followed by the lower leg, the foot, and the upper leg.

A popular new approach to running is barefoot training. Some fitness professionals feel we spend too much time wearing shoes and thus it weakens the foot and leg structures. To strengthen these structures try walking barefoot around the house and perhaps start a barefoot training program. Here's how to go about it.

Developing a Barefoot Running Program

Step 1. Begin by doing different activities of daily life without shoes such as gardening, walking to the mailbox and barefoot walking around the house.

Step 2. Next, do some exercise activities on an even grass surface or indoor surface. Perhaps do some walking, jogging, calisthenics and games (e.g., volleyball or frisbee) on a grass field or indoor track.

Step 3. Try doing 10 minutes of brisk barefoot walking before and/or after a regular workout.

Step 4. Gradually start doing 5-minute bouts of barefoot running before and after a regular workout.

Step 5. Increase slowly from 5 minutes to 10 minutes to 15 minutes of barefoot running before and/or after a regular workout.

Step 6. For variety, do your barefoot training indoors and outdoors (grass and/or sand).

Step 7. Progressively transition barefoot training to a harder surface (such as a side walk) with brisk walking. However, be very aware of rocks, glass and harmful surface disturbances such as holes and rough spots.

Step 8. Cold environments can be a deterrent to barefoot training. Perhaps the use of a fitness facility, indoor location, mall or school gymnasium (where the temperature is more reasonable) would be much more suitable during inclement weather conditions.

Step 9. Importantly, injured runners should not begin doing any barefoot training until the symptoms of their injury have subsided. Also, barefoot running is not recommended for people with diabetes because there may be a loss of protective sensations in the feet with this disease.

Step 10. Several shoe companies are now promoting new 'barefoot' shoes that protect the foot from harmful surfaces. Many people prefer this option for their barefoot training. Give it a try . . . you may enjoy it.

Stretch Right!

A well-designed flexibility program focuses on all the muscle groups and joints of the body—not just the most frequently used body parts. Stretch properly to achieve maximum flexibility.

Stretching Tips

► Stretch warm muscles, not cold ones.

► Avoid bouncing (ballistic) movement. Stretch gradually into and out of the stretch.

► Stretch to the point of limitation, not to the point of pain.

► Concentrate on relaxing the muscles being stretched; slow breathing helps.

► Stretches to improve flexibility should be held 15 to 30 seconds.

► Always stretch opposing muscle groups.

► Keep the muscles warm when stretching by wearing warm-ups or sweats.

► Stretch daily and certainly after every workout.

► Increases in flexibility take time; you must be patient.

Neck

Action: Very slow circular movement of head toward each shoulder and chest.

Tips: It is not recommended to take your head back too far—you may possibly stress your neck.

Shoulders (Two stretches)

1. **Action:** Holding a towel or rope over your head, stretch the arms back.

2. **Action:** Sit on the knees with the front of the feet flat on the floor. With towel behind back, bring the chest to the knees as you stretch the arms away from the body.

Tips: This is also a very good stretch for the spine and the front of the lower leg!

Variation: Change the width of your grip on the towel.

Hips, Side, and Back

Action: While sitting, bring one leg over other leg. Keep the bottom leg extended (but relaxed at the knee). Rotate the torso to both sides by pushing against floor with hands.

Tips: Stretch up through your spine.

Lower Back

Action: While lying on the back, grab behind the knees and pull legs toward chest. May be done with legs tucked or slightly extended, but not locked.

Tips: This also stretches the hamstrings.

Variation: This stretch can be performed in the seated position.

Abdominals and Chest

Action: From a prone position, lift the shoulders and chest off the ground and support the upper torso with elbows or extended arms.

Tips: Reach up and out with the upper body.

Seated Butterfly Stretch
(For inner thigh)

Action: Bring both heels together and into body. Press knees toward the floor.

Tips: Grab your ankles, not your toes. Stretch torso forward as well.

Half-Straddle Stretch
(For hamstrings and lower back)

Action: With one leg straight and the other leg bent, reach your chest forward toward the straight leg and hold. Do both legs.

Tips: Keep the back straight and relax.

Straddle Stretch
(For hamstrings, inner thigh, and lower back)

Action: Stretch forward with your upper body between your open legs.

Tips: Keep your knees facing up, legs straight, and back straight. Placing your hands on the floor behind your thighs is a good modification for those a little less flexible in this position.

Quadriceps and Hip Flexors

Action: While lying on your side, grab below the knee and stretch the leg back.

Tips: Focus on bringing the leg back and not out to the side.

Variation: Do the stretch standing against a wall, next to a chair, or in the prone position.

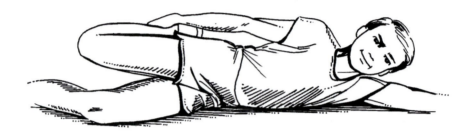

Achilles Stretch and Calf-Stretch

Action: Stand in a lunge position with toes facing forward. To stretch the calf, bend front leg and keep back leg straight. To stretch Achilles tendon (and soleus), bend the back knee, keeping the heel on the floor.

Tips: Sometimes it is best to do these against the wall or an immovable object.

Mind-Body Fitness

What Is Mind-Body or Mindful Fitness?

The fitness industry's growth in the past 15 years has included many new dimensions in programming. Several of these innovative programs distinctively address an area of interest referred to as 'mind-body' or 'mindful' fitness. Mindful fitness is described as increased mental development and personal enlightenment through the participation in some form of movement that includes muscular strength, flexibility, balance, and coordination. With mind-body fitness modalities, the exerciser attempts to blend a mindful or cognitive process with some type of physical movement of low-to-moderate postures or exercise intensity. Mind-body fitness is performed with an inwardly directed focus. Attention of the practitioner is on breathing, posture and body awareness throughout all physical movements. Whereas any traditional cardiovascular and resistance exercise program may include inner-focus elements, with mind-body exercise this inner-attentiveness is the predominant theme throughout the exercise. In mind-body exercise, participants emphasize more effort on self-monitoring, self-awareness and perceived exertion as opposed to following the commands of the certified exercise leader. Thus, with mind-body exercising, the inner-focus elements are the process and the end product. Tai Chi and yoga are influential foundations of the evolving mind-body fitness programs. Because of the lower intensity demands of mind-body exercise programs, they have a wide-reaching adaptability for persons of multiple fitness levels and bodily movement challenges.

Results of recent research indicate there is considerable and meaningful evidence supporting several mind-body programs for interventions with cardiac rehabilitation, insomnia, headaches, incontinence, chronic low back pain, symptoms of cancer and post surgical outcomes. However, more research is needed to understand the mechanisms of these interventions so that specific factors may be identified for clinical use with clients suffering some of these health consequences.

Characteristics of Mind-Body Exercise Programs

Traditional exercise programs focus attention on some type of performance-oriented outcome such as muscular strength, muscular endurance, flexibility, body composition change or cardiorespiratory endurance. The following are five common components of mindful exercise programs.

1. **Meditative/contemplative.** This represents a non-judgmental, present-moment introspective component. It focuses on the moment and is non-competitive.

2. **Proprioceptive awareness.** Proprioception is characterized as a sense of movement and position of the body, especially the limbs. Proprioceptors are sensory organs (such as muscle spindles and Golgi tendon organs) that are capable of receiving stimuli originating in the muscles or tendons. Much attention in mind-body fitness programs is developing this sense with the muscles as the body goes through directive movement.

3. **Breath-centering.** Interests in evaluating and understanding the biological mechanisms associated with breathing are ongoing. The breath is a centering activity in mindful exercise. It comes from the word 'pranayama', loosely translated, the science of breath. Many of the mind-body disciplines include various breathing techniques.

4. **Anatomic alignment** (e.g., spine, pelvis, etc.) or proper physical form. With the various mind-body disciplines, body position, technique and alignment are centermost to the correct performance of the postures. In many ways, this is very analogous to the importance of body position and technique regularly incorporated in performing stretching and resistance exercises.

5. **Energycentric.** Energycentric is a descriptive mindful exercise term used to characterize the perception of movement and flow of one's energy force. This type of positive energy is inclusive in most mind-body programs.

Yoga for Mind, Body, and Spirit

Though its exact origin in India has yet to be identified, yoga has existed for at least 3,500 years. Translated, yoga means union and refers to one of the classic systems of Hindu philosophy that strives to bring together and develop the body, mind, and spirit. Hindu priests who lived frugal lifestyles, characterized by discipline and meditation, originally developed yoga. Through observing and mimicking the movement and patterns of animals, priests hoped to achieve the same balance with nature that animals seemed to possess. This aspect of yoga, known as Hatha yoga, is the form with which Westerners are most familiar and is defined by a series of exercises in physical posture and breathing patterns. Besides balance with nature, ancient Indian philosophers recognized health benefits of yoga, including proper organ functioning and whole well-being. These health benefits have also been acknowledged in the modern-day United States, with millions of individuals regularly participating in yoga.

There are several different forms of Hatha yoga that are popularly practiced. Iyengar yoga incorporates traditional Hatha techniques into fluid and dancelike sequences. It uses props such as chairs, pillows, blankets, and belts to accommodate persons with special needs. Ashtanga yoga is a fast-paced, athletic style that is the foundation for the various power-yoga classes. These classes resemble more vigorous workouts as opposed to relaxation sessions. Bikram, or hot yoga, is done in a sauna-style room that's over 100 degrees, so the muscles get very warm for extending and stretching. Jivamukti is both physically challenging and decidedly meditative. Kripalu yoga centers on personal growth and self-improvement. Although each type of yoga will have its unique benefits, documented benefits from participation in yoga include the following:

► Increase in flexibility

► Increase in muscular endurance

► Increase in balance

► Improvement in posture

► Increase in caloric expenditure

► Increase in self-worth and self-control

► Reduction of stress

The Pilates Method of Movement Training

The Pilates Method was developed by German immigrant J. H. Pilates in the early 20th century. Pilates is a methodical system of slow, controlled, specific movements that involve a deep internal focus. This method is essentially divided into two modalities, floor or mat work and the work on the resistance equipment that Pilates developed, such as the Universal Reformer. Equipment is generally learned in a one-on-one or small group setting whereas mat work can be taught in either a group or private setting. With either modality, but especially with the Reformer, the principle goal is to achieve efficient functional movement and improved movement capability. In many ways, Pilates is a form of movement re-education where each participant learns to overcome faulty compensatory movement patterns. These inefficient movement patterns are broken down into components by using springs (using a Reformer) and changing the body's orientation to gravity. Pilates exercises are designed to enhance more efficient movement patterns by placing the student in a position that minimizes undesirable muscle activity, which can cause early fatigue and lead to injury. Pilates equipment was constructed to adapt to many human anatomical variations. For example, the springs, ropes, and foot bar of the Reformer can be adjusted such that similar properties of movement sequencing can be applied to a variety of body types and limb/torso lengths. Pilates work involves substantial mental focus with harmonized breathing during the muscular contractions of the movements. The Pilates method may be utilized for rehabilitation, post-rehabilitation, general fitness and athletic performance. Pilates exercise is advantageous for those who desire low-impact exercise to improve posture, flexibility, and functionality. Research shows that various Pilates programs can be beneficial in improving flexibility, core strength, muscular fitness and increased caloric expenditure.

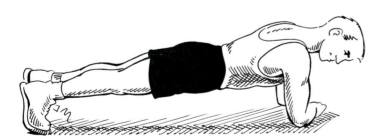

Did You Know?

Each brain cell can communicate with 25,000 other brain cells.

Section 5

Contemporary Health Issues

Striving to be the healthiest person you can be is a very important goal in life. Your pursuit of optimal health emphasizes positive lifestyle practices and prevention strategies. Good health is determined by many of the choices you make in life about exercise, nutrition, weight management, alcohol use, smoking, substance use or abuse, and relationships. Developing your mind and managing your emotions are also closely interrelated with attaining optimal well-being. It is important that you take self-responsibility by engaging in activities that can positively affect your health. You deserve the opportunities that accompany good health. The purpose of this section is to briefly address some meaningful issues to help you make appropriate decisions regarding your personal health and well-being.

Wellness

Closely associated with optimal health is the concept of wellness. Wellness is an ongoing process of becoming aware of and making choices toward a healthy, fulfilling quality of life. Here are some of the different dimensions of wellness.

1. Social wellness emphasizes your interdependence with others.

2. Physical wellness encourages consumption of healthy foods, participation in activities that lead to optimal health (including exercise and self-care) and avoidance of unhealthy lifestyles (such as smoking and drug abuse).

3. Emotional wellness is the degree to which you feel positive and accepting about your own feelings. It includes your ability to realize your potential, your limitations and how you effectively cope with stress.

4. Intellectual wellness supports your pursuit of creative, stimulating activities and mental well-being.

5. Spiritual wellness involves seeking meaning and purpose in your life.

6. Occupational wellness emphasizes your preparation for a career that will provide enrichment and satisfaction.

7. Environmental wellness includes your respect for nature and the many species living in the world.

Self-Concept

Self-concept is how you feel about yourself. It is meaningful to note that someone with a low self-concept is more likely to adopt an unhealthy behavior such as smoking, alcohol, or substance abuse. A person's self-worth should come from the strength of his/her internal resources. Oftentimes an individual lets outside factors such as work, sports, school, or relationships determine his/her self-worth. This is very risky because these factors may be destructive to your self-concept. You need to acknowledge, to yourself, that you have positive attributes as well as faults, and that these qualities should not affect the decisions you make regarding your health. Clarify those physical, emotional, mental, and spiritual needs that must be met for you to be happy. Try to establish a link between your health behaviors and the fulfillment of these needs. This will help provide the direction and motivation for you to realize and sustain positive health outcomes.

> **Did You Know?**
>
> It takes blood 23 seconds to circulate through the body at rest.

The Balanced Eating Plan

Include a variety of wholesome foods in your total dietary intake. "Wholesome food" refers to food consumed in its natural state (or as close to its natural state as possible and free of additives, preservatives, or artificial ingredients) such as baked potatoes versus potato chips, raw fruits and vegetables instead of cooked and canned varieties, and whole-grain breads and cereals as compared to refined products. Processing often removes important nutrients. The best way to obtain the most vitamins and minerals is to eat food in its natural form.

Components of a Well-Balanced Diet

The balanced diet contains adequate amounts of carbohydrates, protein, fats, vitamins, minerals, and water.

Carbohydrates

Carbohydrates are the primary and most easily utilized source of energy for your body. Approximately 58 percent of your total caloric intake should come from carbohydrates. Refined and simple sugars, starches (complex carbohydrates), and fiber (cellulose) are the three forms in which carbohydrates are found in food products. Refined sugars should be limited to approximately 10 percent of your daily carbohydrate intake. Complex carbohydrates, in the form of starches and naturally occurring simple sugars, should comprise the 48 percent balance of caloric intake from the carbohydrate food group. These are readily found in whole-grain breads, vegetables, and fruit. Your body uses carbohydrates, in the form of glycogen and glucose, to provide the energy for moderate, prolonged, and intense exercise and to contribute to the maintenance and functioning of your nervous system. In addition, under normal conditions, carbohydrates are the only energy source for your brain.

Proteins

Proteins are important for the healthy building and repair of every cell of your body. The essential amino acids, which cannot be manufactured within your body, must come from dietary sources. Americans tend to consume about twice as much protein as they actually need. Among key points to remember regarding protein are the following:

1. Proteins are important in helping to maintain your body's water balance.

2. Proteins in the blood help keep the acid level of the blood within a normal range.

3. Proteins are essential for you to have an immune response. This response produces antibodies to foreign substances that get into your system.

4. Many of your hormones are either protein or have protein components.

5. All of the many enzymes of your body are proteins.

6. Proteins act as carriers for a number of substances in your body.

7. Proteins play a role of passing information across spaces between nerves and muscles.

Fats

You need some dietary fat and cholesterol to provide insulation, for energy, for the production of hormones, for absorption of certain vitamins, and as a vital component of cell membranes. The biggest dietary challenge for most Americans is to reduce fat consumption. Total dietary calories from fat sources should be no more than 30 percent of daily food intake. Fats come in three important dietary forms: saturated, monounsaturated, and polyunsaturated. Saturated fats are found in animal products, including meats, poultry, and dairy products such as milk and cheese. Tropical oils, such as palm oil, are predominantly saturated fat and are found in many prepared products. Saturated fat intake should be limited to less than 10 percent of daily caloric intake. The monounsaturated fats such as olive oil and polyunsaturated fats such as sunflower oil should comprise 10 percent each of daily caloric intake.

Unfortunately, elevated blood levels of fat have been linked to diseases of the cardiovascular system and to some forms of cancer. The typical American diet contains >40 percent of calories from fat. The process of reducing this level is difficult and probably more likely to be successfully changed when done slowly. However, the results in potentially better health are well worth the effort invested.

Did You Know?

Twelve percent of caloric intake should come from protein sources containing the essential amino acids.

Water

Water is your most vital nutrient. More than 70 percent of muscle is water, whereas only 10 percent of body fat is water. Water is an important constituent of all body cells. It surrounds the cells, permeates bone tissue, and is the foundation element of the circulatory system. Among its important functions are transportation of nutrients, removal of the by-products of cell metabolism, temperature regulation, joint lubrication, and cell structure shape. In addition, water is a medium for life-sustaining chemical reactions in the body. Drink an average of 8 to 10 eight-ounce glasses of water a day.

Vitamins

A well-balanced diet does not have to be supplemented to meet the daily vitamin requirements. However, a deficiency of one or more vitamins will result in some kind of symptom or deficiency reaction, whereas too much of a vitamin may cause a toxic reaction. Vitamins are grouped into two groups based on their solubility. There are the water-soluble vitamins (B vitamins and C) and the fat-soluble vitamins (A, D, E, K). Toxicity is more likely to occur with fat-soluble than with water-soluble vitamins. The best way to get vitamins in your body is from the foods you eat. Avoid low-nutrient foods like soft drinks and foods high in calories and fat. Nutrient-dense foods like whole grains and fresh fruits and vegetables will provide adequate daily caloric intake, as well as vitamins and other micronutrients. Beliefs that extra amounts of certain vitamins will give extra energy, reduce stress, prevent a variety of ailments, or improve endurance have not been proven by controlled research.

Minerals

The minerals, or micronutrients, are inorganic substances that your body needs in small amounts each day. They facilitate numerous functions in your bodily processes such as enzymatic activities, electrolyte balance, and fluid transport. They also have structural roles in the body.

Following are some general eating guidelines to help you design your all-around best-balanced eating plan.

Diet Guidelines

Meat and Protein Foods

▶ Eat less red meat; reduce the serving size and frequency.

▶ Eat fewer processed and cured meats (like ham, bacon, sausage, frankfurters, and luncheon meats high in saturated fats, sodium, and artificial preservatives).

▶ Select lean cuts such as eye round, sirloin tips, shoulder, chuck, flank, tenderloin, and remove all visible fat before preparing.

- ▶ Eat poultry (white meat without the skin), which has less saturated fat and fewer calories than beef or pork.

- ▶ Eat fish, which is low in fat. However, tuna, salmon, and sardines canned in oil contain more fat and less protein, so purchase them canned in water.

- ▶ Nuts and seeds are rich sources of vegetable protein but also contain a high concentration of calories and fat (mainly the "good" polyunsaturated kind). Sunflower seeds, sesame seeds, walnuts, almonds, and peanuts are the best sources.

- ▶ Although eggs are an excellent source of high-quality protein, the yolks contain a concentrated source of fat and cholesterol. Limit intake to three or four eggs a week, or eat only the whites of the egg.

Dairy Products

- ▶ Eat reduced- or nonfat dairy products such as skimmed milk, low-fat cottage cheese, plain yogurt, and low-fat cheeses. Reduce the amount of cream, ice cream (ice milk has about half the fat of ice cream), whole milk, whipped cream, and cream cheese. These products contain excess fat and calories.

Fats and Oils

- ▶ Use more polyunsaturated vegetable oils such as safflower, corn, and sunflower.

- ▶ Margarines high in polyunsaturates (usually the softer kind) are preferred.

- ▶ Avoid hydrogenated or trans fats (processed fats that are more saturated such as buttery crackers, french fries, fish sticks, and pastries).

- ▶ Avoid palm oil and coconut oil, which are also high in saturated fat.

Fruits and Vegetables

- ▶ Eat raw fruits and vegetables daily. Many vitamins and minerals are destroyed in the cooking process.

- ▶ Eat dried peas and beans, which in their natural state are excellent lowfat sources of protein.

Breads and Cereals

▶ Eat whole grain breads and cereals, rather than refined ones. During the refining process, essential "B" vitamins and minerals are removed along with the bran (the outer layer of wheat kernel). Vitamin E is also lost when the wheat germ is expelled. Enriched breads and cereals replace many (but not all) of the lost nutrients.

Healthy Eating Tips

▶ Avoid eating large meals. A large meal elevates blood sugars and fatty acids. This extra food will usually be stored as fat in your body. Eat small meals at more frequent intervals throughout the day.

▶ Foods that are cooked, stored in the refrigerator (or freezer), and then reheated later lose many of their vitamins.

▶ Eat slowly and chew your food completely. Fast eating encourages overeating.

▶ Avoid overusing the salt shaker.

▶ Limit consumption of cookies, cakes, and candies; they contain excessive amounts of sugar and fat.

▶ Read the label panels of foods to evaluate the nutrient content and look for hidden ingredients.

▶ Include more fiber in your diet. The typical American diet is too high in calories, sugars, fats, and sodium.

▶ Drink no more than two cups of coffee a day to avoid symptoms of anxiety such as nervousness, irritability, increased blood pressure, muscle tension, and difficulty sleeping.

▶ Avoid skipping meals (especially breakfast). Many times when meals are skipped, people more than make up for it at another meal.

▶ Spread your toast and bread with fruit-only jams instead of sugary jellies and butter.

▶ Satisfy your sweet tooth with low-fat treats such as frozen juice bars, nonfat yogurt, fresh fruit, and angel food cake.

▶ Toss your salad with gourmet vinegar and herbs instead of regular dressing.

▶ Eat air-popped popcorn at movies or for a snack.

▶ When buying peanut butter, choose the natural-style and pour the oil off the top.

▶ Use nonfat milk instead of cream or nondairy creamers in coffee.

► Give yourself permission to eat moderate amounts of the foods you enjoy on a regular basis.

► Get plenty of fiber. It is associated with lowered risk for cancer, diabetes, and coronary artery disease. Increase the amount of oats, beans, lentils, fruits, and vegetable skins.

► Add peanut butter and peanuts to your diet. Although there are fats in peanut butter, they are mostly monounsaturated while also being high in folic acid, thiamin, vitamin E, niacin, magnesium, zinc, and protein.

The Chocolate Fallacies

Everyone is entitled to enjoy eating chocolate in moderate amounts. However, some manufacturers would like to convince you that eating chocolate is more for health than pleasure. Here are some chocolate fallacies.

Fallacy #1: Eating chocolate doesn't make you fat.

In reality, no one single food does cause obesity. However, chocolate is a food with a lot of calories, so it is important to watch how much you eat for agreeable weight control.

Fallacy #2: Chocolate protects the heart.

It is true that one of the saturated fats in chocolate, called stearic acid, doesn't raise cholesterol. But chocolate has other saturated fats, such as palmitic acid, that do raise cholesterol. Also, it is meaningful to mention that stearic acid may help to promote blood clots, which can trigger heart attacks and strokes.

Fallacy #3: Chocolate helps to prevent cancer.

Chocolate does contain a high level of antioxidants, which are protective molecules for some cellular functions. Presently, many studies show the link between fruits and vegetables and a lowered cancer risk, but the studies on chocolate and cancer risk reduction are not here yet.

Bottom Line

For many of us, chocolate is a sweet sensation that is an utter enchantment for our culinary desires. In moderation, it certainly provides great fulfillment, with few harmful effects. It may be a wonderful delight, but at this time no research suggests it is a wonder food.

Welcome to "MyPlate"

The 'Food Guide Pyramid' has now been replaced with the new "MyPlate" food guide plate. The new icon consists of a dinner plate divided into four slightly different-sized quadrants and an 8-ounce glass of milk (which also could be cheese or yogurt). Fruits and vegetables occupy half of the dinner plate, with grains and healthy proteins occupying the other 50 percent. Please notice that the vegetable portion is slightly larger than the fruit portion and the grains portion is a little bit bigger than the proteins portion. This is certainly easy to understand. And, if you to want modify your diet, the new United States Department of Agriculture (USDA) web site (www.ChooseMyPlate.gov) is a useful resource. Spend some time and read through the site and you will understand more about making healthy food choices for your personalized diet. The website for "MyPlate" offers readers a number of useful diet tips, such as healthy eating tips, interactive diet planning, weight-loss information and more. It also provides links to things such as a database of farmers markets and government nutrition information.

Some of the messages of this new healthy-eating initiative by the USDA are straightforward such as enjoy food, but eat less and make half your plate fruits and vegetables. The USDA is encouraging you to drink water instead of sugary drinks and switch to fat-free or low-fat (1%) milk. As well, the USDA is encouraging you to reduce salt intake and continue limiting your intake of saturated and trans fats.

This visual plate concept is really helpful because it allows everyone to easily assess their meals without trying to measure portion sizes or count calories. It is a very clear tool that is promoting balance, portions, variety and wholesome foods for each meal.

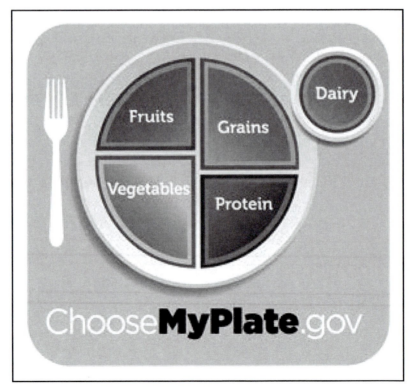

Source: http://www.choosemyplate.gov/

Reading Food Labels

Most foods in the grocery store must now have a nutrition label and ingredient list. Reading the new food label will help you choose healthy foods for your diet. Here are what some key words now mean on product labels as defined by the government.

Fat Free	Less than 0.5 gram of fat per serving
Low Fat	3 grams of fat (or less) per serving
Lean	Less than 10 grams of fat, 4 grams of saturated fat and 95 milligrams of cholesterol per serving
Light (Lite)	One-third less calories or no more than one-half the fat of the higher-calorie, higher-fat version; or no more than one-half the sodium of the higher-calorie version
Cholesterol Free	Less than 2 milligrams of cholesterol and 2 grams (or less) of saturated fat per serving
Note: g = grams (abot 28 g = 1 ounce) mg = milligrams (1,000 mg = 1 g)	

Make sure you check to see if your serving is the same size as the one on the label. If you eat double the serving listed, you need to double the nutrient and calorie values. If you eat one-half the serving size, cut the nutrient and calorie values in half.

Let the Daily Value be your guide. Daily Values are listed for people who eat 2,000 or 2,500 calories each day. If you eat more, your personal daily value may be higher than what's listed on the label. If you eat less, your personal daily value may be lower. For fat, saturated fat, cholesterol, and sodium, choose foods with a low % Daily Value. For total carbohydrate, dietary fiber, vitamin, and minerals, your Daily Value goal is to reach 100 percent of each.

Nutrition Facts

Serving Size ½ cup (114g)
Servings per container 4

Amount Per Serving

Calories 90	Calories from Fat 30

	% Daily Value*
Total Fat 3g	5%
Saturated Fat 0g	0%
Cholesterol 0mg	0%
Sodium 300mg	13%
Total Carbohydrate 13mg	4%
Dietary Fiber 3g	12%
Sugars 3g	
Protein 3g	

Vitamin A	80%	Vitamin C	60%
Calcium	4%	Iron	4%

* Percent Daily Values are based on a 2,000 calorie diet. Your daily values may be higher or lower depending on your calorie needs:

	Calories	2,000	2,500
Total Fat	Less than	65g	80g
Sat Fat	Less than	20g	25g
Cholesterol	Less than	300mg	300mg
Sodium	Less than	2,400mg	2,400mg
Total Carbohydrate		300g	375g
Fiber		25g	30g

Calories per gram
Fat 9   •   Carbohydrate 4   •   Protein 4

More nutrients may be listed on some labels.

Weight Management

Obesity has risen to epidemic levels in the U.S., with over 67% of the U.S. adults being overweight or obese. Obesity is highly associated with type 2 diabetes and coronary heart disease, and also increases the risk for high blood pressure, stroke, gallbladder disease, osteoarthritis, sleep apnea, respiratory problems, and some types of cancer. In addition, overweight and obesity and their associated health problems have a significant economic impact on the U.S. health care system.

> **Did You Know?**
>
> Statistics estimate that 40 percent of all women and 25 percent of all men in the United States are on a diet.

Many weight-loss programs have directed their weight management interventions toward one single proposed cause of obesity. However, for long-term weight management, integrating several interventions will attain the best success.

What is the Energy Balance Equation?

Ultimately the primary reason for overweight and obesity is a positive **energy balance** input (via foods consumed) versus a lower energy expenditure output (via physical activity and exercise). Thus, for overweight and obesity to develop, the energy balance is disrupted when food intake over-matches the body's energy output in physical activity. Energy balance means that energy intake equals energy output. We have evolved with an outstanding ability to biologically function with great energy efficiency by storing large amounts of excess fat intake into fat tissue. In the current society, many people spend hours watching TV, playing games on computers, doing sedentary schoolwork, and adopting other leisure activities.

Our present food abundant circumstances may be a by-product of our success as a society, but it clearly creates an energy imbalance in our lifestyle. Other environmental factors contributing to obesity include not having enough sidewalks, trails, parks and affordable fitness facilities for all people. Restaurants, fast food places, movie theatres and recreational outlets often compete for our business with their huge, oversize food portion offerings. Lastly, healthy food choices are more expensive, making access to these foods less of an option for the financially challenged.

Factors Influencing Obesity

Obesity may be defined as the percentage of body fat equal to or greater than 25 percent for men and 32 percent for women. It is associated with increased risk of cardiovascular disease, hypertension, diabetes, gallbladder disease, and certain cancers. Obesity appears to be influenced by

1. decreased physical activity,

2. high-fat diets,

3. genetics and,

4. behavioral factors.

A better understanding of these factors may help you design a favorable weight-loss plan.

Physical Activity

Physical activity has changed dramatically as our nation has evolved from an agricultural to industrial to technological society. Clearly 32.7 percent of adult Americans are completely sedentary, and 20.3 percent are inadequately active. This slump in physical activity has resulted in a significant decrease in daily caloric expenditure for the majority of Americans.

> **Did You Know?**
>
> According to the Center for Disease Control (CDC), only 47 percent of Americans engage in leisure-time physical activity at the level recommended for health benefits.

High-Fat Diets

Diet composition is now high in fat and refined sugar and low in starches and fiber. It is well documented that humans gain weight on high-fat diets. As a matter of fact, dietary fat is converted to body fat with approximately 25 percent greater efficiency than carbohydrates. Factors affecting this increased fat intake are expert retailers' pushing foods high in fat and sugar, fast-food restaurants, vending machines, and the fact that Americans are eating out more often.

The Genetic Factor

The distribution of body fat in the body, principally in either the upper or lower body, is an inherited trait. Extra fat in the torso is associated more with men and increased health risk, whereas overfatness in the hips is associated more with women. If both parents are obese, it's very likely their offspring will also be overweight. Although the trend to develop obesity may be inherited, regular physical activity combined with a lower calorie diet will definitely limit this genetic tendency if maintained throughout the life cycle.

> **Did You Know?**
>
> The average percentage of fats in the American diet is about 43 percent, although the recommended percentage is 30 percent or less.

Your resting metabolic rate is also a distinctive bodily process influenced by genetics. The resting metabolic rate (the energy required to maintain vital bodily functions including respiration, heart rate, and blood pressure) accounts for 60 to 75 percent of your daily energy expenditure. It may vary considerably between persons. For instance, the resting metabolic rate may differ by as much as 1,000 calories a day in obese women of the same height, weight, and age. In addition, investigations have shown that individuals with low metabolic rates gain more weight than persons with normal resting metabolic rates. The resting metabolic rate of women is about 5 to 10 percent lower than males because of less muscle mass.

Fat cell number is another genetic factor that influences obesity. The average person has 25 to 35 billion fat cells in the body. Some obese individuals have up to three times the normal fat cell number. An individual experiencing continual weight gain may also produce more fat cells during adulthood. Unfortunately, once new fat cells have developed, a loss of fat will only result in a decrease in size but not number, leaving the individual with a higher number of fat cells. Mildly obese or overfat individuals usually have a normal fat cell number. Weight gain in this case is associated with an increase in size and weight of fat cells.

Behavioral Factors

A number of the pioneer studies investigating the caloric intake of obese to nonobese subjects have revealed no appreciable difference in caloric intake between the two groups. However, new studies using technologically superior techniques for measuring caloric intake have shown that obese subjects typically underestimate their caloric intake by 30 to 35 percent. In fact, modern hospital- and university-based weight management investigations report binge eating disorders in 25 to 45 percent of obese individuals. Studies also show a strong link between psychological stress and binge eating. The implication of these results supports the importance of learning healthy eating habits as well as keeping accurate food inventories for persons in a weight-management program.

High-Protein, Low-Carbohydrate Diets: Debating the Diet Wars

Information technology is bombarding us with confusing and conflicting reports on what is the best way to achieve permanent weight loss. Some diets now being touted are the high-protein, low-carbohydrate diets, which are in direct opposition to the recommendations of the majority of health, nutrition, and fitness professionals. Leaders in the high-protein, low-carbohydrate diets include Dr. Atkins's New Diet Revolution, The Zone, Protein Power, and the Carbohydrate Addict's Diet. These diets assert that cutting carbohydrates is the key to weight loss, because carbohydrates elevate your insulin levels, and insulin is a fat-producing hormone, converting blood sugar to stored fat. This statement is physiologically correct. The rise in insulin is the body's way of sending the blood sugar (glucose) to the brain and muscles for energy, with unused glucose being stored as fat. Low carbohydrate advocates claim that by limiting the intake of carbohydrates, you avoid the rapid rise in blood sugar, which means less sugar will be stored as fat.

Other respected scholars argue that weight gain is more a function of consuming extra calories, regardless of the type of food (fat, carbohydrate, protein). They state that many people, when advised to eat more carbohydrates and less fat, take that as a message to eat as many carbohydrates as they desire. This "ticket to eat" inference has led many people into just eating more calories than they are expending, thus ensuring unwanted weight gain.

So why do people lose weight on these high-protein, low-carbohydrate diets? Some health professionals argue that the reason for the rapid weight loss in the high-protein, low-carbohydrate diets is attributable to a striking loss of water weight. This occurs for two reasons:

1. The body stores 3 parts of water to 1 part of carbohydrate. Significantly reducing carbohydrates will dramatically lower your water (not fat) weight.

2. By eating more proteins, the body's protein metabolism is enhanced, which requires the use of extra water for elimination of its byproducts.

Some researchers suggest that people are essentially just eating fewer calories on these high-protein, low-carbohydrate diet plans. Another possibility is that eating extra protein actually helps to curb your appetite, assisting you to eat less.

The high-protein, low-carbohydrate diets also claim that the body will more readily break down fat for energy over carbohydrates. This hypothesis hasn't been validated in studies, however.

Researchers have also studied high-carbohydrate, low-fat, and very low-fat diet regimes. These style diets have been very successful for people striving to lose weight. It is important to note that the carbohydrate selections include more vegetables, fruits, grains, brown rice and beans, as opposed to french fries, cakes, and soda. They also promote fat-free yogurt and skim milk or their soy versions.

What about people who are insulin resistant? In the United States, approximately 10 to 25 percent of the population suffers from insulin resistance. These individuals are more susceptible to heart disease due to elevated blood fats, high blood pressure, and lower HDL (helpful) cholesterol. When insulin-resistant people consume carbohydrates, their insulin levels go up, but the body has difficulty utilizing the sugar for energy. Therefore some "experts" suggest these individuals should just eat fewer carbohydrates. However, reducing body weight and increasing physical activity are much more preferable ways to treat people with insulin resistance. Research has clearly shown that aerobic exercise and resistance training are very effective in improving one's sensitivity to insulin. Exercise promotes an efficient uptake of glucose for fuel. So, what should you do?

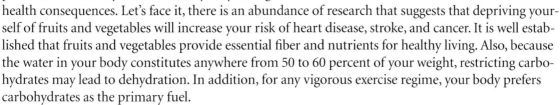

Although people can lose weight on the high-protein, low-carbohydrate diets, they may have grim health consequences. Let's face it, there is an abundance of research that suggests that depriving yourself of fruits and vegetables will increase your risk of heart disease, stroke, and cancer. It is well established that fruits and vegetables provide essential fiber and nutrients for healthy living. Also, because the water in your body constitutes anywhere from 50 to 60 percent of your weight, restricting carbohydrates may lead to dehydration. In addition, for any vigorous exercise regime, your body prefers carbohydrates as the primary fuel.

Perhaps, the best diet is one that does not wipe out carbohydrates, fats, and animal foods and is based on good old-fashioned serving sizes—eating in moderation. This may not result in the fastest loss of weight, but it is an attainable lifestyle for many that will in the long run lower your risk to coronary artery disease, diabetes, stroke, and some forms of cancer.

The Stress, Cortisol and Obesity Story

Today there are several products that tout the effectiveness of cortisol-combating supplements that propose to help people lose weight and feel less stressed by inhibiting the effects of cortisol. Cortisol has definitely become the 'prime-time' hormone of fascination, mystery and confusion within the consumer industry, due to these misleading advertisements. It is a steroid (compound based from a steroid nucleus) hormone that is produced in the cortex of the adrenal glands located on top of each kidney. Exercise, fasting, food intake, and chronic life stressors cause the body to release cortisol. Cortisol regulates foodstuffs by helping to select the type and amount of substrate (carbohydrate, fat or protein) that is needed by the body to meet the

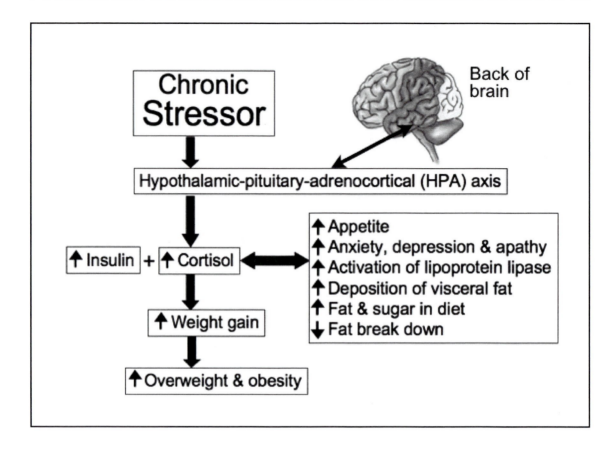

demands placed upon the body's systems. Cortisol also mobilizes energy by tapping into the body's fat stores and moving it from one location to another, or delivering it to hungry tissues such as working muscle.

With chronic stress the hypothalamus (which is the central control station for stress) directs the pituitary gland (below the hypothalamus) in the brain to send a signaling message hormone (known as adrenocorticotrophic hormone or ACTH) to the adrenal cortex (outer portion of adrenal glands on the kidneys), which results in the release of cortisol (see Stress, Cortisol and Obesity Pathway figure). This reaction is referred to as the hypothalamic-pituitary-adrenocortical (HPA) axis, and it is most active during the early morning hours in humans. If the chronic stress (whether real or perceived) is of sufficient magnitude and duration the HPA does not wind down, as it should, resulting in a prolonged period of time that cortisol is elevated. Thus, chronic stress leads to daily increases of cortisol secretion. Cortisol is known to stimulate appetite during the intermittent recovery periods while a person is experiencing chronic stress in their daily life. Cortisol, with the help of slightly elevated insulin levels, has also been shown to activate lipoprotein lipase, the enzyme (lipoprotein lipase) that facilitates the deposition of fat. In the presence of slightly higher insulin levels, elevated cortisol promotes the storage of fat. Thus chronic stress consistently contributes to greater fat accumulation in the trunk area, which is called visceral fat. So, cortisol really isn't the problem! Stress is the problem. See the section on Stress Maintenance on how you can beat stress.

Ten Strategies for Weight-Loss Success

Americans spend over $35 million dollars a year trying to lose weight. It's no secret that diet books, diet pills, packaged foods, liquid diets, weight-loss groups, and hospital-sponsored programs abound, and yet at this junction in time no single program, plan, or treatment offers long-term effectiveness to large numbers of individuals. A winning weight-loss program will not be as concerned with loss of weight as it is with loss of body fat. Follow these tips for weight-loss success.

1. **Don't go on a crash diet or fast.** Very low calorie diets, often referred to as crash diets, lead to quick loss of muscle and fat. Only a small number of dieters will reach their goal weight, and fewer than 5 percent will maintain their new weight. Fasting exposes the body to a condition that actually increases the activity of fat-depositing enzymes. Your body is reacting to what it perceives as starvation conditions and tries to protect itself from not being supplied the necessary foodstuffs.

2. **Go for fat loss—calories count!** The best diet to promote fat loss is a well-balanced, low-fat, heart-healthy, high-carbohydrate eating plan composed of a variety of foods to ensure good nutrition. It is important to educate yourself on which foods are high in fat and which are low. A rule of thumb for caloric expenditure is to consume roughly 16 calories per pound for moderately active people and no less than 1,200 calories a day. A high-carbohydrate, low-fat diet is also recommended for lowering the risk of high blood cholesterol, coronary artery disease, and high blood pressure.

3. **Exercise works.** The exercise program is essential to the success of any weight management plan and should be composed of aerobic exercise and resistance training. New research shows that persons who "Accumulate" 250–300 minutes of aerobic exercise during the week have the greatest weight loss success. This research shows that you can accumulate this total amount (250–300 minutes per week) in as little as 10-minute bouts of moderately intense exercise spaced throughout the days of the week. Of course, everyone is encouraged to gradually work up to this total amount of aerobic exercise per week. In addition, resistance exercise has been shown to impressively maintain your muscle mass during weight loss interventions. Thus, you will be preserving the most adaptable and metabolically active tissue in your body—muscle!

   Did You Know?

   The cell structure of your skeleton rejuvenates itself completely every 10 years.

4. **Food choices.** Choose food that is low in calories but high in nutrients. Eat more complex carbohydrates such as whole-grain breads, cereals, rice, vegetables, bran products, and oatmeal. Substitute sugar-rich desserts with fruits. Drink plenty of water. It is a major component of your body and provides the environment within which the other nutrients may function. Eat low-calorie, nutrient-dense foods for snacks to help control your hunger between meals. Watch your consumption of alcohol. Alcohol has plenty of calories, but no nutrient value. Limit your salt intake to that which occurs naturally in food.

5. **Weight-loss goals.** Establish safe weight-loss goals. A loss of up to two pounds per week is a healthy recommendation for weight loss. Avoid seeking that slender fashion model figure. This may be too unrealistic and could lead to psychological distress and diet failure.

6. **Eating habits.** Many people eat till they are too full, mainly because the food tastes so good. Take responsibility and use good judgment at your meals. Also, it is not healthy just to eat when you are hungry. Instead of two or three large meals a day, eat five or six smaller ones, which better distributes your caloric needs throughout the day. Eat at a slower pace to avoid overeating and stomach discomfort.

7. **Food doesn't solve problems.** Unfortunately, conditions such as stress, emotional distress, or loneliness may lead some individuals to use food as a way of dealing with the problem. Attempt to disassociate food with these issues and seek professional counseling if necessary to establish appropriate intervention strategies. Food is an enjoyable fuel for life, not a mood-heightening support system.

8. **Behavior modification.** A major goal of any successful weight management program is to modify behaviors that may contribute to the problem. Begin by identifying those factors that may reinforce behaviors that are counterproductive to your body fat goals. Two helpful behavior modification measures involve the application of knowledge and values. Knowledge of accurate nutrition and exercise information is invaluable to complete your successful plan. Establishing new values enables you to develop behaviors that improve your quality of life and attain your body fat goals. Maintaining a positive attitude will certainly help.

9. **How to choose a good diet.** Choosing a safe and effective diet may be difficult with the hundreds of "miracle" diets on the market. Avoid programs that advertise unique fat-burning enzymes or fat-reducing formulas, as no known substances or formulas exist. Stay away from the quick and easy promises—there is no fast and easy way to lose excess fat. Steer away from those one-food diets, as they are deficient in essential nutrients. The program should be low in calories but complete in essential nutrients. It should incorporate a variety of food choices that you enjoy. Make sure the diet fits into your way of life. It should be designed to reduce no more than two pounds of fat per week. Finally, the diet you select should have lasting potential. Ask yourself if you can maintain it for a lifetime.

10. **Lifetime changes.** The dietary, exercise, and behavior changes you make should be sustainable for a lifetime. Develop a faithfulness and appreciation for exercise and health, not an obsession with thinness.

A 'N.E.A.T.' New Idea for Weight Control

As obesity in children and adults continues to rise, there is a pressing need to develop new combating strategies. A new line of research is looking at the role that standing, walking, moving, and fidgeting plays in combating weight gain and obesity. As such, a relatively new component of energy expenditure is N.E.A.T., which stands for non-exercise activity thermogenesis (a physiological process that produces heat).

N.EA.T. comprises the energy expenditure of daily activities such as standing, walking, talking and sitting—all activities that are not considered planned physical activity of a person's daily life. Some professionals refer to N.E.A.T. as spontaneous physical activity. To measure NEAT investigators use sensitive physical activity monitoring inclinometers and accelerometers that can be worn on the hips and legs of the body.

Research findings are showing that obese persons tend to sit 2.5 hours more than their lean counterparts on a daily basis. Video games, television, spectator sports events, computer entertainment and a sedentary lifestyle contribute to this seated behavior. As well, much of our daily life is now completed at seated workstations.

Many teachers and fitness professionals are now helping students learn how to incorporate more movement in their daily activities. The theme is 'move more and sit less'. Here are 15 ideas you can try to add more movement in your own life.

1. Walk during your lunch hour

2. Take a family walk after dinner

3. Walk your dog

4. Replace the Sunday drive with a Sunday walk

5. Go to the park and play

6. Run or walk fast when doing errands

7. Every time you take a coffee, tea or water break take a walk break

8. Always walk as you talk on your cell phone

9. Start gardening

10. Walk briskly when at the store or in a mall

11. Walk up the stairs instead of the escalator

12. Go for a hike

13. Begin dancing more often

14. Go for a ride on your bike

15. Do your home cleaning more frequently

Substance Abuse

Alcohol

The costs of alcohol problems in America have been estimated to exceed $70 billion per year, with the majority of these costs attributed to reduced productivity. It is second to tobacco as the leading cause of premature death.

Some general reasons people drink alcohol:

▶ It often serves as a medium for friendship when people meet "for a drink."

▶ It is frequently used to celebrate an event.

▶ It is a means of dealing with stress, anxiety, emotions, or depression.

▶ It is commonly used in social situations to lessen fears and make people feel at ease.

▶ It is a lure successfully used by clever advertisers.

▶ It is a behavior often introduced by role models.

Did You Know?

Alcohol is indicated in nearly half of all deaths caused by motor vehicle crashes and fatal intentional injuries such as homicides and suicides.

Alcohol Continuum

Researchers have identified an alcohol continuum from which people may be able to evaluate or assess themselves or others.

▶ An *occasional drinker* drinks in small amounts, usually on special occasions.

▶ A *light drinker* drinks regularly in quantities that are not intoxicating.

▶ A *social drinker* drinks moderately, but in quantities that are not intoxicating.

▶ The *problem drinker* drinks to the point of intoxication, following no specific pattern or even realizing what is happening.

▶ The *binge drinker* drinks heavily. Usually the drinking is linked to issues arising at work, home, or within his/her social life.

▶ The *chronic alcoholic* has problems associated with long-term, uncontrolled, and frequent drinking.

Women and Drinking

A variety of unique problems may arise when women drink. Females tend to have more body fat than men, and alcohol concentrations tend to be higher in people with more body fat. With less muscle mass than men and less water in their tissues (fat tissue has very little water), alcohol is absorbed into the bloodstream faster, even when all other absorption variables are constant. Therefore, a man and woman with the same body weight, who have consumed the same amount of alcohol in the same time period, will find the woman to be more intoxicated (primarily due to her body fat content). The negative effects to the fetus of a mother who drinks are well documented. Fetal alcohol syndrome is the second-highest cause of mental retardation in the United States. This is entirely preventable!

Drink Responsibly

The amount of alcohol in a person's bloodstream at a given time is referred to as one's blood alcohol concentration (BAC). The liver metabolizes 0.5 ounce of alcohol per hour. This is equivalent to the following drinks: 12 ounces of beer, 12 ounces of a wine cooler, 5 ounces of wine, or 1.5 ounces of liquor. It takes approximately one hour for any of these drinks to be metabolized by the liver and the BAC to return to normal. If more alcohol is consumed than is metabolized, the BAC will rise, and signs of impairment in motor skills, speech, equilibrium, and decision making will increase accordingly.

It is your responsibility to keep your BAC low and your behavior under control. Be aware of the reasons you may be drinking and make responsible decisions of how much you drink, what you drink, your limitations, your attitudes toward others who drink, and the consequences associated with alcohol use.

Tobacco

One out of every six deaths may be attributed to smoking. The use of tobacco is closely linked to diseases of the cardiovascular system, a number of cancers, respiratory infections, and ulcers.

The active ingredients in smoking tobacco are nicotine, tar, and carbon monoxide. Nicotine, which is extremely addictive, stimulates the production of epinephrine. This causes the blood pressure and heart rate to increase and blood vessels to constrict. Tar, similar to that on city streets, is a sticky fluid that settles in the lungs and inhibits their functioning. Carbon monoxide is a deadly gas that retards the effective transportation of oxygen through the bloodstream.

Did You Know?

According to the Surgeon General, smoking is the single-most important preventable cause of death in the United States.

The rate of female smokers is on the upswing whereas it is decreasing for the rest of the population. This increase in women smokers has been attributed to a desire of some females to have a slender image. This same desire makes it very difficult to quit smoking, as there usually is a small gain in weight that accompanies smoking cessation. The important point to stress is that smoking is a far greater risk to a person than gaining a few extra pounds.

Tobacco is consumed in five different forms:

1. cigarettes

2. low-tar and nicotine cigarettes

3. clove cigarettes

4. cigars and pipes

5. smokeless tobacco

Although the low-tar and nicotine cigarettes are proposed to be safer, many of these smokers actually increase their cigarette consumption to satisfy their need for tar and nicotine. Smokeless tobacco (snuff or chewing tobacco) use is increasing, especially among young males. It is not a safe alternative for people who wish to quit smoking. Cancer of the cheek and gums is 50 times higher among smokeless tobacco users.

To quit smoking is a difficult process that requires breaking both a psychological and physical addiction to nicotine. It is very difficult for smokers to quit on their own. There are several programs available that utilize a number of approaches (behavioral, psychological, sociological, and pharmacological) that have proven to be successful in helping people stop smoking. With the cessation of smoking, a number of positive improvements in health rapidly occur. These include:

► improvement in sense of smell and taste,

► more efficient food digestion,

► better circulatory and cardiorespiratory function,

► better heart efficiency,

► improvement in breathing capacity.

Other Drugs

Drug use can be found throughout every area of the country, in all social levels, at all income levels, and within many group affiliations. It is associated with a number of health problems including overdoses, drug-related violence, injuries, HIV infection (from shared needles), and birth defects. Oftentimes the use of drugs begins with harmless curiosity and results in substance abuse and dependence. Signals of drug dependence include the following:

1. emotional withdrawal,
2. decline in academic performance,
3. loss of interest in usual activities,
4. change in social groups,
5. concern with obtaining money, and
6. cranky behavior.

There are several categories of substance abuse drugs, which include the following.

▶ **Psychedelics.** The psychedelics or hallucinogenic drugs produce sensory and perceptual distortions of reality that may be pleasant or terrifying. Many of these drug episodes will last up to 12 hours and cannot be ended early.

▶ **Opiates.** Heroin, long a part of the drug world, has similar but more powerful pain-relieving properties than morphine. Its main ingredient is opium, which is very addictive.

▶ **Central nervous depressants.** Barbiturates are central nervous system depressants that may depress muscle control, speech, anxiety, and mood.

▶ **Central nervous stimulants.** Cocaine and amphetamines are central nervous system stimulants. Amphetamines are occasionally used to curb appetite and to cope with difficult situations, such as cramming for tests. Babies of women who are cocaine users during pregnancy are more likely to have birth defects. Stimulant drugs often result in behavioral disturbances, irritability, hostility, and unprovoked violence. It should be noted that caffeine and nicotine are also central nervous system stimulants.

▶ **Marijuana.** Marijuana is probably the most used illegal drug in the country. Attempts have been made to legalize it, with activists proclaiming marijuana less dangerous than tobacco or alcohol. However, the smoke in marijuana is harmful to the respiratory system. Although the long-term use of marijuana is unknown, chronic use of marijuana has been associated with infant mortality and neurological problems.

▶ **Deliriants.** Designer drugs fall into this class. These are illegal drugs intended to replace some of the various street drugs.

A variety of programs are accessible to help people break their drug habits. Many treatment programs use substitution drug therapy. Counseling and support groups are also available. The most desirable solution to drug abuse is prevention. There are numerous ways to enjoy the gratification of a healthy life without having to depend on the dangerous stimulation of drugs.

Stress Maintenance

Stress is an inevitable part of living. When you feel too much stress you react with the "flight or flight response." This is the body's automatic response system that prepares you to "fight" or "flee" from an actual or perceived threat. A Harvard physiologist discovered the "fight or flight response." He describes it as a protective mechanism that is hard-wired in our brains. However, excessive stress and burnout can have emotional consequences.

One of the main causes of stress is a sudden, drastic, unwanted change: personal loss in the family, a job crisis, injury or illness, financial problems, and emotional problems all fall into this category. The tension from stress often leads to the worried, uptight sensation we call anxiety—you feel angered or frustrated. If these feelings continue to obstruct your ability to enjoy life, physical ailments such as ulcers and high blood pressure may result.

Being "stressed-out" may even lead to depression. Do you recognize the symptoms of depression?

▶ restlessness

▶ feelings of inadequacy and insecurity

▶ inability to concentrate

▶ sleeplessness

▶ lack of interest in food, life, and social interaction

Did You Know?

The right side of the brain is the control center for creative thinking.

You can beat it! You can take charge!

Follow these guidelines:

1. Talk over your problems with a close friend or seek professional advice. You need to express your feelings!
2. See a physician if you have any physical ailments.
3. Do vigorous exercise regularly to vent anxiety and to combat depression.
4. Don't overload yourself. Set practical goals you can reach successfully and timetables you can meet.
5. Learn to relax. You need some peace and quiet each day just for **you!**
6. Organize your work and personal affairs. This will give you more efficient use of your time and will rid your life of clutter.
7. Take short breaks or a vacation. Time out will give you a better perspective.
8. Look ahead. Sometimes you can anticipate a job slump, a budding problem, or financial difficulties and be prepared.
9. Stay away from drugs and alcohol—they are just temporary relievers of tension, not cures for problems.
10. Improve your eating habits and your diet. Don't skip meals because you are too busy.

Stress Release Breathing Intervention

Here's a simple breathing drill you can do anytime to help lessen the effects of stress. Sit very comfortably and focus on relaxing your muscles in your body, especially those that are tensing up. Keep your breathing very slow and controlled. As you inhale say to yourself, "I am," and as you exhale say to yourself, "relaxed." Continue for 3 to 5 minutes.

Technology to Technostress

Although the benefits of technology are enormous, a new, unexpected type of stress is technostress. Technostress is the anxious feeling one gets by feeling reliant on technological devices (computers, fax machines, voice mail, remote control devices, cell phones, etc.). Thanks to technology, more people than ever before are adopting sedentary lifestyles, while spending hours at a time on a computer.

What Are Some Symptoms of Technostress?

A common symptom is diminished concentration. People feel as though their memory is failing them, forget what they started to do, misspeak words, can't find the right words, or lose their train of thought. Impatience and irritability are also other symptoms. When you are technostressed it is difficult to find time to relax.

So, What Are Some Technostress Busters?

One simple suggestion is to go outside for a walk. Just being in the outdoors, in nature, appears to be most beneficial. Start an outdoor hobby such as gardening, hiking, or biking. All types of exercise are beneficial including aerobic exercise, resistance training, and flexibility training.

Avoiding Burnout

Everyone has the potential to suffer from burnout. The end result is a diminished capacity to function efficiently. Oftentimes the high demands needed for success, criticisms from others, and unrealistic expectations are underlying themes for burnout to occur.

How to Avoid Burnout

1. Be careful of working extra long hours; in the long run this can lead to fatigue and loss of motivation.

2. Overextending yourself: try not to solve all of the world's problems. Get involved, but be realistic about your capabilities.

3. Too much stress, frustration, and anxiety in your daily life may lead to burnout.

Signs of Burnout

1. Attitude shift toward negativity; you may start putting less effort in current projects or an indifference toward your work.

2. Exhaustion; look for signs of frequent illnesses, fatigue, or even sadness.

3. Feelings of inadequacy; you may feel moody and less competent in areas in which you are really more talented, educated, and skilled.

Some Ways to Reduce Burnout

1. Be a good listener to your body. If you are regularly ill, exhausted, and fatigued, your body is warning you that something is wrong.

2. Realize you cannot do everything and be realistic on what you can accomplish.

3. Examine your work hours and perhaps incorporate some time-management strategies.

4. Don't overbook yourself.

5. Learn something new. Sometimes the boredom of work can take its toll. Go to some guest lectures or a seminar on a topic of interest. Pick up a new book to read.

6. Do something different. Perhaps you might find much satisfaction in having a pet or starting some type of hobby. Be willing to try something you've always considered, but never felt you had the time to do.

7. Do something different in your job. If possible try to do something different in your job that breaks you from the mode you might be experiencing. Students might want to buy some new video learning aids now available in most college bookstores.

Finally, try to draw a line in your life from who you are and what you do. Allow time for some of your friendships to grow and reestablish your lifestyle values for home and happiness.

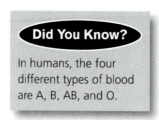

Did You Know?

In humans, the four different types of blood are A, B, AB, and O.

The Eight Energy Bolsters

Do you ever get that feeling you want more energy? Do you know what to do? Here are some simple but effective tips you can do to bolster your energy.

1. Start by eating healthy and enough. Oftentimes the restrictive diets people attempt lead to early fatigue and low energy. Also, these same diets are often deficient in important vitamins and minerals your body needs to stay healthy.

2. Drink more water. A good rule of thumb is to drink about 1/2 to 1 cup of water every hour you are awake.

3. Get your carbohydrates. Without a doubt, carbohydrates are the most influential nutrients that regulate your energy. Eat plenty of whole-grain breads and cereals, rice, potatoes, pasta, and beans.

4. Take your vitamins and minerals. You may wish to consider a multivitamin if you know your daily diet seems insufficient. Key vitamins to focus on are vitamin C, calcium, magnesium, and potassium.

5. Keep an eye on iron. It is no secret that iron deficiency is a prevalent cause of fatigue in women. Don't forget that tofu and kidney beans are good sources as well as lean red meat.

6. Don't skip breakfast. Breakfast will help maintain your blood sugar levels that have dropped from your previous evening of sleep.

7. Sleep on. It is important to get the adequate sleep your body needs. Losing only one or two hours can sometimes sap you in the day and lead to weight gain.

8. Exercise. Aerobic exercise and resistance training improve several metabolic processes that can all lead to increased energy.

Creative Problem-Solving

Whether it's solving a school issue, a personal challenge, or a family dilemma, resolving a problem can be quite stressful. When faced with this type of task, use these 10 ways to help resolve your predicament.

1. **Clearly define the problem.**

2. **Explore all possible solutions.**

3. **Be positive** and optimistic that you are going to successfully resolve this issue.

4. **Discuss and analyze** this problem and possible solutions with others who you respect. Choose colleagues who show a sincere interest in your well-being.

5. **Don't be overly critical** of any resolution ideas.

6. Allow yourself to **be imaginative** during this process.

7. Sometimes a new or different solution makes you feel apprehensive. **Feel confident** that it is OK, because you are using a fresh problem-solving approach.

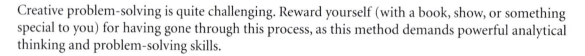

8. **Summarize your options.**

9. **Choose a resolution** direction and put it into action.

10. **Observe and evaluate.** If the problem is not resolving, you may need to try another one of your options.

Creative problem-solving is quite challenging. Reward yourself (with a book, show, or something special to you) for having gone through this process, as this method demands powerful analytical thinking and problem-solving skills.

Time Management Tips

Let's face it, time management for everyone can sometimes get pretty outlandish. With personal responsibilities, family responsibilities, work responsibilities, school responsibilities, and much more to do, it is no wonder many people find themselves overloaded. Use these eight tips to help you anticipate, organize, and take charge of your time.

1. **Start a master schedule.** Write down all your goals, commitments, and things to do. Make sure this master schedule is updated daily. This is also a good time to evaluate whether you have taken on too many projects and need to "put something on hold" for a later date.

2. **Organize and prioritize** your goals and commitments. Now that you have a master schedule, prioritize everything to keep you on track. Allow this organizational process to be very fluid, as goals and objectives often shift in importance.

3. **Focus on the big picture.** It is easy to lose a lot of energy micromanaging things that are of less importance. Focus your attention on what needs to be accomplished, in the order you have established.

4. **Be wary of regular distractions.** Telephones, pagers, cell phones, and e-mail can become distractions to accomplishing tasks. Sometimes it is best to allocate priority work times when you will not accept incoming communications and other possible distractions.

5. **Project breakdown.** Many people find it more productive and efficient to break down a large task into miniprojects.

6. **Establish a realistic time line for projects.** This may be the most difficult step. However, by creating a realistic time line you are helping yourself to avoid procrastination.

7. **Be an "objective detective" time manager.**
An objective detective time manager can regularly anticipate the unexpected, such as more time needed for an assignment, and readjust his/her master schedule accordingly.

8. **Block into your life some daily "flex time."** Try to have some time each day that is allocated flex time to take care of projects that need more time or for you to get ahead on other coursework.

Be a Great Communicator

Life is a constant state of communication with friends, colleagues, employers, teachers, and others. Here are eight suggestions to improve your professional and personal relations by being a more effective communicator.

1. Look at the other person. Always **make eye contact** with the person you are communicating with in a live conversation. This reflects self-confidence on your part.

2. **Listen actively** to the other party. Focus on the conversation without thinking of other things.

3. **Stay on track.** Some discussions start to digress when one or both parties begin to bring up unrelated issues or pointless past events.

4. **Avoid being judgmental.** Always try to be objective and comprehend the other person's point of view.

5. **Be sensitive and respectful.** In all conversations and discussions, appropriate respect and sensitivity to the feelings of others is appreciated.

6. **Clarify and then repeat.** Try not to assume anything in a conversation. Clarify important points and repeat statements to verify that what you heard was correct.

7. **Observe body language.** Oftentimes others may project their feelings with their body language. Observe the hands, face, and posture, and note how this person is expressing himself or herself nonverbally.

8. **Be supportive and constructive.** In all conversations make a point to be constructive and supportive in your feedback.

Save a Life: Be a Stroke Detector

Most people do not know how to detect a person having a stroke, and yet every minute an American has one! Presently, with proper response time, medical researchers have developed helpful drugs that can resolve the clot causing the stroke. Here are the signs of someone having a stroke.

1. Sudden severe headache with no known cause

2. Unexplained dizziness or sudden falls

3. Some loss of vision, particularly in one eye or experiencing double vision

4. Sudden difficulty speaking or understanding speech

5. Sudden weakness or numbness of the face, arm, or on one side of the body

What Can You Do to Prevent a Stroke?

Each of us can take steps to prevent a stroke for loved ones and ourselves. An important first step is to lower blood pressure if it is too high. Do at least 30 minutes of moderate intensity exercise daily. If overweight, lose weight and eat plenty of fruits and vegetables daily. Smoking really increases the risk of stroke due to the noxious chemicals in smoke that make the blood vessels stiffer. If you smoke, STOPPING may save your life. You can prevent a stroke from occurring with your positive approach to a healthy lifestyle!

Exercise Improves Brain Function!

Most recently, research on the favorable effects of exercise and brain function is emerging. Studies with physically active women and men indicate they have much less cognitive decline when they exercise regularly. Some scientists believe that physical activity may impart a neuroprotective effect in the brain, boosting brain health and cognitive (thinking, reasoning, remembering, imagining or learning) functioning.

The majority of the exercise and brain function research has been done using cardiovascular exercise as the intervention, and it is considered the most important form of exercise for improved brain function. Aerobic exercise induces the formation of new blood vessels in the brain during childhood and adulthood and improves brain circulation for better oxygen and nutrient delivery. In addition, programs combining aerobic exercise, resistance training and flexibility are quite effective for cognitive function improvement, although the underlying mechanisms why are speculative at this time. Doesn't this brain and exercise research make you want to workout?

Ten 'Fascinating' Facts about the Brain

Here are some interesting bits of information about the brain.

1. That brain is 75% water.

2. The average number of thoughts that you experience each day is about 70,000.

3. Every time you blink, the brain 'kicks in' to keeps things illuminated so the world doesn't go dark during the blink (which we do about 20,000 times a day).

4. While awake, your brain generates between 10 and 23 watts of power—or enough energy to power a light bulb.

5. You can't tickle yourself because the brain can distinguish between unexpected touch and your own touch.

6. Excessive stress can alter brain cells, structure and function.

7. The brain uses about 20% of the total oxygen of the body at rest.

8. You continue to make new neurons throughout life as long as you use your brain in mental activities.

9. There are about 100,000 blood vessels in the brain.

10. The average brain, which weighs about 3 lbs, has approximately 100 billion neurons.

Sleep: A Gift to Your Body and Mind

Scientists suggest that sleep provides the following 3 major functions: 1) it serves as the energy restoration (recharging) period from the daytime activities, 2) it affords bodily protection at night when sensory capacities are down-regulated, and 3) sleep affords the brain needed time to consolidate important experiences and memories for learning. Most men and women need 7–8 hours of sleep a night. Chronic sleep debt is commonly defined as sleeping between 4 to 7 hours of sleep a night.

Sleeping Hygiene Tips

The following are sleep hygiene tips to help you get most favorable sleep.

1. Limit naps to a maximum of 30 minutes and try to do earlier in the day.
2. Avoid bringing food to bed.
3. Avoid bringing paperwork and work projects to bed.
4. Create a sleep-friendly bedroom by doing the following: use comfortable linens and pillows, put up darker shades, replace a worn-out mattress, and keep the bedroom cool during sleep.
5. Attempt to deal with stressful issues during the day and put them away at night (seek professional consultation if necessary to better deal with the stress).
6. Drink fewer fluids after dinner so the need to get up to go to the restroom is minimized.
7. Set a regular time to go to bed and a consistent time to awaken, and keep to this schedule.
8. Create a 'noise-free' sleeping environment.
9. Do not smoke or use any other products with nicotine before bed, as the nicotine keeps many people awake. Encourage clients who smoke to quit.
10. Cut down on caffeine consumption in the late afternoon and evening.

Five Vital Facts About Sleep Restriction

1. One-third of U.S. adults report chronic sleep restriction.
2. Chronic sleep restriction is particularly connected to motor vehicle accidents.
3. Sleeping more on the weekends to make-up for a loss of sleep during the workweek is not good sleep hygiene as it disturbs normal sleep-wake cycles.
4. Ever-present sleep restriction is associated with learning and memory loss.
5. Continual sleep restriction is linked to diabetes, depression, hypertension, and cardiovascular disease.

Health Risks of Obesity

Conditions associated with obesity include: diabetes, high blood pressure, sleep apnea, and high cholesterol, some cancers, heart disease, and reduced life expectancy. Even modest weight losses of 5%–10% of initial body weight have positive benefits on coronary heart disease risk factors.

Other benefits of weight loss include:

▶ Enhanced feelings of well-being

▶ Reduced joint pain and improved ease of movement

▶ Increased energy levels

▶ Decreased levels of anxiety and depression

▶ Decreased need for medications

▶ Greater quality of sleep

Energy Balance Equation

Obesity is caused by a complex interplay between genetic, environmental, and behavioral factors. Weight gain occurs when energy intake exceeds energy expenditure as depicted below. Resting metabolic rate, physical activity, and thermic effect of food are the main components of energy expenditure. Disturbances in RMR as a result of sarcopenia (age-related loss of muscle mass) or hypothyroidism may cause the dramatic shift toward a positive energy balance. In addition, physical inactivity can contribute to weight gain, as it reduces the amount of energy expended each day. Other cultural, economic, and behavioral factors may also contribute to the obesity epidemic.

Positive energy balance (Figure 1)

▶ Calorie intake exceeds expenditure

▶ Net result = Weight gain

Negative energy balance (Figure 2)

▶ Calorie expenditure exceeds intake

▶ Net result = Weight loss

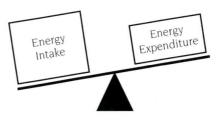

Figure 1
Positive Energy Balance = Weight Gain

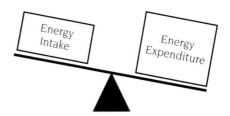

Figure 2
Negative Energy Balance = Weight Loss

What Is Metabolism?

▶ Metabolism is the rate at which your body burns calories.

    ▷ It is the same thing as "energy expenditure" in the energy balance equations.

▶ What components make up metabolism?

    ▷ Resting Metabolic Rate (RMR) = 60–70%

    ▷ Thermic Effect of Food (TEF) = 5–10%

    ▷ Physical Activity Energy Expenditure (PAEE) = 15–30%

▶ Estimating your resting metabolic rate with the Harris-Benedict equation:

    ▷ For men: RMR = 66 + (6.23 × weight in pounds) + (12.7 × height in inches) – (6.76 × age in years)

    ▷ For women: RMR = 655 + (4.35 × weight in pounds) + (4.7 × height in inches) – (4.7 × age in years)

▶ Applying the equation:

    ▷ little to no *exercise* = RMR × 1.2

    ▷ Light exercise (1–3 days per week) = RMR × 1.375

    ▷ Moderate exercise (3–5 days per week) = RMR × 1.55

    ▷ Heavy exercise (6–7 days per week) = RMR × 1.725

    ▷ Very heavy exercise (2x's per day, heavy workouts) = RMR × 1.9

▶ Men naturally burn more calories than women. This may be due to increased activity level and increased muscle mass. Also, RMR tends to decrease with age.

How Can I Improve My Metabolism?

▶ Smaller, more frequent meals

▶ Get plenty of sleep each night

▶ Consume a diet full of nutrient-dense foods, starting with a balanced breakfast!

▶ Begin a balanced exercise routine

    ▷ Strength—increases muscle mass, which increases resting metabolism

    ▷ Aerobic—increases physical activity energy expenditure

    ▷ High intensity interval training—has been shown to elevate EPOC or excess post-exercise oxygen consumption. This refers to the increased rate of oxygen intake following strenuous exercise that is intended to erase the body's "oxygen debt." During the hours that follow exercise, your body is working harder to return back to a resting state and recover from the exercises performed. This results in an increased calorie burn, which researchers have estimated may last up to 24 hours following exercise.

▶ Don't starve yourself

    ▷ Dropping your calorie intake below 1,000 calories a day may signal to your body that you are in starvation mode, and typically slows down your metabolism.

Applying the Science and Seeing Results

▶ You have to burn 3,500 kcals in order to lose 1 pound of fat.

▶ For best results, you should aim to keep weight loss between 1–2 lbs per week.

▶ So . . . to shed 1 pound you would need to create a 500 calorie deficit each day. If you've used the Harris-Benedict equations to estimate your total daily energy expenditure including exercise, then this part is pretty simple, you can either add in more activity to increase your daily calorie expenditure or decrease the amount of calories that you take in (energy intake) or you could do both.

▶ For example, you could burn 250 calories by walking on the treadmill each day and then cut 250 calories out of your daily diet. This would result in the 500 calorie deficit that is needed each day in order to lose 1 pound per week.

The Truth Is. . . .

There is no simple, quick painless way to lose weight permanently. You have to make lifestyle changes a top priority. Here are some strategies to help increase your chances of success:

▶ **Plan exercise into each day.** Habitual physical activity is the number one predictor of long term weight loss maintenance. If you can't do 30 or 60 minutes all at once, then break it into smaller bouts. The American College of Sports Medicine (AGSM) recommends engaging in at least 150 minutes of moderate intensity physical activity each week to help facilitate weight loss and between 200–300 minutes per week to maintain weight loss. Choose exercises that you enjoy! If you struggle with motivation, consider finding an exercise buddy to help keep you accountable.

▶ **Keep daily food logs.** Writing down what you eat each day can help you keep track of your calorie intake, especially as it's easy to ignore a handful of candy here and there or an extra can of pop. This can also be done using a pen and paper or online through free websites such as *www.sparkpeople.com* or using the SuperTracker at *www.choosemyplate.gov.*

▶ **Focus on controlled portion sizes.** By measuring out foods you can better estimate caloric intake. You may want to consider even doing this ahead of time—such as dividing up the leftover grilled chicken into 4 oz. containers so that it is ready to add to your lunch or even make a quesadilla or a salad.

▶ **Get adequate sleep and water intake.** Research has shown that individuals who get 7–8 hours of sleep per night have lower BMI's than those who only get 5–6 hours. Some researchers speculate this may be because sleep deprivation may affect the secretion of the hormone cortisol, which has been shown to increase appetite. Also, adequate water intake is helpful for increasing feelings of fullness, especially between meals.

▶ **Write down your goals.** Be sure to create goals that are specific, measurable, achievable, relevant, and timely. Having an action plan that works for you will help increase your chances of success, just be sure to keep track of your progress and adjust your plan as needed. You may want to consider measuring your progress in more ways than just change in body weight—as the scale alone cannot tell you percent body fat, how many inches you've lost, how much muscle you've gained, and how specific health parameters (i.e., blood pressure) have improved.

Recognizing Fad Diets

Because we are constantly looking for a faster and easier way to lose weight, some diets have emerged that claim to help you lose weight fast or without giving up the foods that you love. These fad diets deceive people into thinking that following them can result in healthy, long-term weight loss.

Here are some common characteristics of fad diets:

▶ They eliminate one or more food groups.

▶ They are not nutritionally balanced.

▶ The advertising is full of testimonials.

▶ They promise rapid weight loss, often with no mention of weight maintenance.

▶ They don't provide unbiased research and are not validated by the scientific community.

▶ They often require the use of special products.

▶ Sales staff are represented as nutrition/medical experts.

▶ They do not encourage exercise or behavior change.

Healthy Weight Gain

▶ Implement a complete, total body strength training program.

▷ Aim for at least 3 sets and 6–10 repetitions to complete or near-complete muscular fatigue, 3 days per week (or more frequently if using a split-routine).

▶ Plan nutritionally balanced menus with adequate food.

▷ Calculate energy needs to ensure that additional calories are consumed.

    ▷   To help facilitate protein synthesis for muscle building, protein intake should be 1.5–2.0 grams per kilogram of body weight.

▶ Incorporate healthy, higher calorie snacks.

    ▷   Nuts, nut butters, low fat cheeses and dairy products may be good options.

Eating Disorders

Anorexia Nervosa

▶ A relentless pursuit of thinness and unwillingness to maintain a normal or healthy weight

    ▷   Weigh less than 85% of what is considered healthy

▶ An intense fear of gaining weight

▶ Self-esteem that is heavily influenced by perceptions of body weight and shape, or a denial of the seriousness of low body weight

▶ Lack of menstruation among girls and women

▶ Highest mortality rate of all psycho-somatic illnesses—20% of anorexic individuals die as a result of their condition.

▶ Enlisting professional help is necessary to treat this illness.

Bulimia Nervosa:

▶ Characterized by binge and purge cycles

▶ May affect as many as 1 in 5 women on college campuses

▶ Those affected may be at or near normal weight

▶ Can eat in excess of 7–10,000 kcal in one binge

▶ Purging may involve vomiting, use of laxatives, or strenuous exercise

▶ Diagnosis criteria:

    ▷   Recurrent episodes of binge eating, lack of control, self induced vomiting or laxative use, twice a week for three months or more

▶ Complications:

    ▷   Change in BMR due to weight cycling

    ▷   Cardiac arrhythmias, ulcers, colitis, tooth erosion, muscular weakness

Food Diary and Food Journal

Use the Super Tracker on the Choose My Plate website. It's easy to use! This site is free to use and contains helpful nutritional information. Just follow these steps:
Go to: *www.choosemyplate.gov*

1. Choose Super Tracker

2. Create a profile. Enter all the information. Register your profile and save your information. Write down your username: _____ and password: _____ ; so you can return to the site. If you don't create a profile, your information will NOT be saved, and you will have to recreate everything the next time you visit the site.

3. Use the top tabs, and choose My Plan. Review the 2000 daily guidelines.

   Print these for your information.

4. Next, choose the Track Food and Activity tab. Choose the Food Tracker and enter all the food you eat for at least one full day.

   Just type in the name of the food, banana, for example. A pop up menu will appear and give you multiple choices on how that banana was eaten. Choose the one closest to the one you ate.

   Choose the amount eaten.

   Choose the meal at which you ate that food.

   Click ADD.

   Repeat this process for all foods eaten that day. For combination foods, such as "pizza," choose combination foods, to get the pop down list with choices similar to the type of food you are looking for.

   Enter at least 3 meals and 1 snack.

   Print the page (you must end up with a detail listing of all the foods you ate).

5. Use the top tabs again, choose My Reports. Choose Food Groups & Calories. Create a report by entering the date for which you entered your food choices (#4 above). Create a PDF file (it gives you this choice). Print this report.

6. Return to the top tabs again. Choose My Reports. Choose Nutrient Reports. Enter the same dates you entered in number #5 above. Create a report. Save it as a PDF file. Print.

   To complete this assignment, you must compare your meal plan with the Basic 2000 calorie plan (#3 above).

   Compare the following things:

   My daily caloric intake was _____

   This amount is over/under (choose one) by _____ calories.

Compared to the targets for each food group, I am over/under (choose one) by:

	TARGET	MY INTAKE	AMOUNT OVER/UNDER
Grains:			
Vegetables:			
Fruits:			
Dairy:			
Protein:			
Oils/Fats:			

7. Using the Nutrient chart (#6 above), list all the nutrients where you did not reach the daily target requirements:

_____

_____

8. Create a Food Journal. Go to the **My Features** tab. Choose Journal. Fill out the foods eaten, where you ate, and physical activity and "mood" sections. Save as a PDF file. Print.

SECTION 6

FITNESS FACTS AND FICTION

Frequently Asked Questions

General Health

1. **Do smokers also have an increased risk of heart disease besides cancer and strokes?** Yes, smokers have more than twice the risk of a heart attack as compared to nonsmokers. The good news is this risk begins to drop as soon as the person stops smoking.

2. **Should men and women take vitamins and supplements for improved health?** It would be preferable to get your nutrients from a healthy, balanced diet, but most research shows that Americans don't get enough of key vitamins and minerals. Consider taking a multi-vitamin. Women may also need to take vitamin D and calcium for the prevention of osteoporosis.

3. **What can a woman do to lower her risk of breast cancer?** Studies show that regular exercise, healthy nutrition, and smoking cigarette cessation are most beneficial. In fact, exercise has a strong inverse relationship with breast cancer. Cancer risk is 25% lower for the most physically active women. Also, being physically active throughout your life confers even greater risk prevention.

4. **Does a high fiber diet prevent cancer?** Many scientists now believe that a high fiber diet will not prevent colon cancer. However, high fiber diets are linked to lower risk of cardiovascular disease and do prevent constipation.

5. **I see some articles that say coffee dehydrates you and other articles that it doesn't. What gives here?** Recently, the Institute of Medicine published some guidelines on hydration and noted that caffeine-containing beverages did not significantly dehydrate people. The belief that for every cup of coffee you consume you need to drink a cup of water is a myth. The guidelines also mentioned that alcohol is not a dehydrating substance. The guidelines state that caffeine, colas, tea and alcoholic beverages (in MODERATION) may help contribute to the body's fluid needs.

6. **Is it true that a person with high blood pressure may have impaired thinking ability?** Yes! Unfortunately people with high blood pressure are more apt to have obstructions or narrowing of the small blood vessels of the brain. A lack of appropriate nourishment to brain cells may rob them of life sustaining nutrients, leading to cell death and possible impaired thinking.

7. **What's the difference in mineral water, sparkling water, spring water and purified water?** Good question. Spring water flows naturally to the earth's surface from an underground formation. This makes up most of the bottled water sold in the U.S. Mineral water is spring water that naturally contains at least 250 milligrams of dissolved minerals (like calcium and magnesium) per liter. Sparkling water is spring water that contains carbon dioxide gas. Purified water has been treated with some type of distillation, reverse osmosis or ion exchange process.

8. **What are four major factors that contribute to improved health?** Regular aerobic exercise, regular resistance training, improved dietary habits, and a positive mental attitude.

9. **Will exercise make you tired?** Only temporarily; exercise will ultimately give you more energy.

10. **Will exercise enhance your sex life?** You bet! Increased energy, more vitality, higher self-esteem, stress control, and body firmness all contribute to a person's sex life. Right?

11. **Will exercise give you a longer life?** The aging process cannot be reversed, but exercise may slow down normal physiological deterioration. More importantly, exercise can improve the quality of your life.

12. **What qualities do people who have lived to be 100 have in common?** Moderation and a positive outlook on life. Few smoke and few are fat. They usually get up early and go to bed early. Many claim to have always kept busy during their lives and describe themselves as hard workers. They all seem to be very self-sufficient and protect themselves from too much stress. Most are active daily walkers who eat a plant-based diet.

13. **How does smoking affect exercise?** Smoking constricts the bronchial tubes, which are the pathways by which oxygen and other gases enter the body. Also, the carbon monoxide in cigarette smoke can combine with hemoglobin in red blood cells, taking space that should be used to transport oxygen to the exercising muscles. Thus, your cardiorespiratory system must work harder to do the same amount of work.

14. **Can exercise really improve your mental health?** Yes, studies have shown that exercise brings about both short- and long-term psychological enhancement and mental well-being. Some of the psychological benefits from physical activity include improvement in self-confidence, relief of tension and feelings of depression, positive changes in mood, increased alertness, clearer thinking, and positive coping strategies. Individuals of all ages and gender can realize these benefits from exercise.

15. **Does the distribution of body fat have any health consequences?** Yes, people who gain fat in the abdominal area have a higher risk of coronary heart disease, high blood pressure, diabetes, some cancers and stroke as compared to individuals who gain fat in the hip area.

16. **Why do people who exercise have fewer colds and viral infections?** It has been observed that exercise may boost the immune system and that physically active people take better care of themselves. It should be noted that regular, strenuous exercise has also been shown to have an opposite effect on the body's immune system. This adds support for an exercise program directed toward regular, moderate levels of exercise participation.

17. **I read a lot about the health benefits of soy. Are they true?** Soy has been shown to be very health beneficial. For instance, research shows that soy consumption will lower triglycerides and LDL-cholesterol (lousy cholesterol) in people with high blood lipids, while raising the HDL cholesterol (helpful cholesterol). Note also that heart disease is much lower in Asian countries, where soy is a dietary staple. Soy also has been shown to play a role in lowering breast and uterine cancer.

18. **How does soy improve one's health?** It is felt that the hormone phytoestrogen mimics some of the effects of estrogen, actually blocking off some of the harmful effects associated with estrogen. Also, remember that soy foods are low in saturated fat and are cholesterol free. For an Internet source on soy-based foods and products, go to www.soyfoods.com.

19. **As you age, is there anything you can do to slow the decline in mental process?** The degree of decline varies from person to person, but the age-related changes are due to alterations in the brain's frontal lobe, right behind the forehead. However, new research suggests that sedentary older people who take up aerobic exercise (such as walking) can slow the loss in mental ability even if they never exercised before in their lives. Researchers believe that the aerobic activity improves mental functioning by increasing the supply of oxygen to the brain.

20. **How health beneficial is massage for backaches?** Research on massage with people who have chronic low back pain shows that one massage a week substantially reduces the pain and improves mobility. Treat yourself to a good massage.

21. **I use a computer everyday. Are there any exercises that will help prevent and control carpal tunnel syndrome?** Carpal tunnel syndrome is a condition that develops from repetitive wrist motions such as typing at a computer terminal. This motion may lead to pressure on the median nerve in the wrist and great pain and discomfort. Do the following exercises throughout the day. Frequently take your wrists through a complete range of motion in both directions. Make a tight fist with both hands, hold for 6 seconds, and repeat 3 to 4 times. Also, circle your wrists in both directions while holding your hands in a fist. Make sure you take short breaks from your typing to do these exercises (and to rest your wrists) to safeguard from developing carpal tunnel syndrome.

22. **What is hypoglycemia?** Hypoglycemia, also called low blood sugar, occurs when blood glucose drops below normal levels. Carbohydrates are the main dietary source of glucose. Rice, potatoes, bread, tortillas, cereal, milk, and fruit are carbohydrate-rich foods. If your blood glucose begins to fall, glucagon, which is another hormone made by the pancreas, signals the liver to start breaking down glycogen and release the glucose into the bloodstream. The symptoms of hypoglycemia include shakiness, nervousness, sweating, dizziness, confusion, difficulty speaking, anxiety and weakness. If you experience these symptoms regularly see your health care provider.

23. **Can you tell me in minutes or days how much smoking reduces life?** According to some research, every cigarette a person smokes reduces his/her life by 11 minutes. Each carton of cigarettes represents a day and a half of lost life. For every year a person smokes a pack a day, it shortens his/her life by about two months.

24. **What's the latest on St. John's wort?** St. John's wort is a very popular "feel-good" herbal supplement. Many people take it to fight depression and lift their spirits. The scientific evidence is quite convincing that it is effective for treating *mild* depression for a short period of time, around two months.

    Alas, there is no evidence that it will elevate your mood if you are not mildly depressed, so don't rush out to buy it in hopes of making you feel more cheery. Most studies with St. John's wort have lasted no longer than 6 weeks, so the long-term benefits are really unknown.

    Lastly, St. John's wort may lessen the effect of certain medications, so always speak to your physician or a pharmacist before taking this herbal supplement.

25. **What should you look for when buying a new pair of sunglasses?** Sunglasses shield your eyes from dust, wind, ultraviolet (UV) rays, and glare. Look for the Z80.3 sticker that ensures the shades protect against all types of ultraviolet light. Sunglasses labeled "cosmetic use" and "general purpose" usually offer less protection. Surprisingly, the tint has nothing to do with the protection; it's the chemical coating in the lens that blocks the UV rays. However, brown, gray, and green are pretty much the best colors for general-purpose vision because they don't distort colors. For skiing, boating, and sports where light is reflected, you probably need special-purpose sunglasses, which block UV and a lot of visible light. The plastic and polycarbonate lenses are better at blocking UV rays then untreated glass. Plus, they are impact-resistant. Although comfort and style will always be important in your choice, try to select sunglasses that don't block your peripheral vision; safety should always prevail over outward show.

26. **How are colds and flu viruses spread?** Cold and flu viruses are usually spread by shaking hands with the infected person or by touching something the infected person recently held. You will infect yourself by then touching your mouth, eyes, or nose. To prevent exposure, wash your hands regularly when around people with colds and flu viruses. Also, coughing and sneezing can transmit viruses, so keep your distance from those who are ill.

27. **What's the most common joint injury people have in the United States?** According to the American Academy of Orthopaedic Surgeons, ankle sprains are the most common joint injuries. Your ankles are regularly transmitting forces equal to three to four times your body weight when you run and jump. Up to 85 percent of the ankle injuries are inversion sprains. This is when the sole of the foot turns inward, injuring the ligaments on the outside of the ankle. As with any joint injury, the symptoms are pain, tenderness, and swelling. Remember, treatment for sprains is R.I.C.E.: Rest, Ice, Compression, and Elevation.

28. **Is there any merit to these hair analysis ads to detect nutritional deficiencies?** Don't be wowed by these ads. Your hair is predominantly a protein called keratin, plus some small amounts of fat and melanin, which gives your hair its color. Hair analysis cannot detect nutritional deficiencies or detect any diseases for that matter. Your hair does not contain any vitamins, and the mineral levels are not realistic values to measure for any health assessment.

29. Is second-hand smoke dangerous? Absolutely! Second-hand smoke accounts for at least 53,000 deaths in the U.S. It has a surprising consequential impact on coronary risk, even after only brief encounters. Some of the "toxic" effects of second-hand smoke include an increase of the blood to clot, impaired functioning of blood vessels, lowering the HDL (healthy) cholesterol and elevating the LDL (lousy) cholesterol. Besides increasing the risk of lung cancer and respiratory disorders, second-hand smoke may have adverse effects on a woman during pregnancy.

30. Does cold weather give you colds? People exposed to chilling temperatures often feel they are more susceptible to colds. However, viruses give you colds, not the weather. Colds are actually more common in cold weather because people are inside more, and thus more exposed to germs.

31. How do you avoid repetitive strain injuries? With the wonderful benefits of computer use, there are also some physical perils to know. Repetitive strain injury (RSI) results from hand, wrist, arm, and neck injuries from a repetitive (fast) work. Carpal tunnel syndrome is a form of RSI that results from pain in the tendons and nerves across the wrist. To avoid, take frequent breaks during your typing and make sure your computer set up avoids any neck, back, wrist, and eye strain (see *Sitting at Your Computer Station* on page 43).

32. Are the sunless tanning lotions safe? According to the U.S. Food and Drug Administration they are safe. The main ingredient in self-tanning products is dihydroxyacetone, which reacts with the top layer of skin to form a light brown tan stain. Remember that these lotions do not give you any sun protection, however.

33. How successful are all the stop smoking interventions? The interventions range from acupuncture, nicotine gum and patches, hypnotism, antidepressants, and behavior modification approaches. None of the methods has outstanding long-term effects, with each method showing a 20 percent success rate after one year. Quitting smoking is essential. A person needs the support of the family and friends as well as a sustained effort to find the intervention that works.

34. What causes your limbs to "fall asleep"? A limb will become numb when you remain seated or lying in a position that compresses a nerve in the limb or stops the blood flow to the nerve. This sometimes happens when you cross your legs or arms for an extended period of time. When you remove the pressure, the tingling is the nerve sensitivity returning. Moving the limb helps to speed up the recovery. Men who carry a thick wallet in their back pocket (with tight pants) can put pressure on the sciatic nerve, causing a similar numbness and pain.

Exercise

35. I do aerobics and resistance training in the same workout. Which sequence is better—aerobics first or resistance training first? Good news, science suggests that doing either of these types of exercise first has a different physiological advantage. One investigation has clearly shown that aerobic exercise using the same muscles that will be trained in the resistance exercise can lessen (not by much) the amount of work completed during the resistance exercise. So, if you cycle before you do a leg workout, this may slightly impair your leg workout. However, cycling before upper body exercises will not impair your workout. Yet another recent study shows that doing aerobics prior to resistance training will elicit a slightly greater post-workout caloric expenditure—you may burn a few more calories using this sequence. Best advice—vary your sequence.

36. There seems to be a lot of debate as to whether pre-workout stretching has any effect on reducing injuries. What is the best recommendation? This answer is still being debated. Importantly, a good warm-up is probably more imperative than stretching for the prevention of injuries in most exercises and sports. Let's face it, a good warm-up increases blood flow to muscles, enhances oxygen and foodstuffs to the working muscle while it simultaneously removes waste products. And it improves blood viscosity within muscle. Animal studies suggest a good warm-up increases muscle elasticity, which decreases the likelihood of muscle injures. Focus on a thorough warm-up before your workout and complete your stretching for muscle elongation after your workout.

37. I'm confused! After reading all of the harmful effects of obesity, I now see articles that say you can be Fit and Fat! Where is the line here? People who are slightly or moderately overweight but NOT OBESE can be fit if they exercise regularly and eat a healthy diet. If a person has borderline to high blood pressure, elevated blood sugar, or abnormal cholesterol levels, then one of the helpful health suggestions is to lose some weight. For most people, a little overweight is not a health problem, except that it often leads to gradual weight gain.

38. I understand there is new research on lactic acid or the "burn" during exercise? What is it? During intense exercise the development of the "burn" in muscle, referred to as acidosis, has been traditionally explained as an increase in the body's production of lactic acid. This "lactic acid" cause of acidosis is taught in many physiology, biochemistry and exercise physiology courses throughout the world. The most recent research shows that lactate production is ACTUALLY A CONSEQUENCE of cellular acidosis and NOT the cause of the acidosis. More blatantly, lactate production actually RETARDS ACIDOSIS. Lactate is a temporary 'neutralizer' or 'buffer' to the cells elevated accumulation of protons during high-intensity exercise. Lactate production is therefore considered good and not bad for contracting muscle. Lactate is not a bad molecule, and it has been given a bad rap by being falsely blamed for the cause of the burn.

39. Should you exercise on hot, humid days? Keep it light. Sweat will not evaporate well (to cool you off) in the humidity, and you may overheat.

40. Are those so-called "sports drinks" beneficial during exercise? The composition of these drinks is basically water, electrolytes (minerals capable of carrying an electrical charge), and glucose. Sweat consists mostly of water and electrolytes. In prolonged endurance events, glucose (carbohydrate) replacement may be beneficial. Also, endurance exercise in heat contributes to heavy losses of water and electrolytes, which need to be replenished.

41. Is it OK to drink water while exercising? Yes, your body's circulation system must get food and nutrients to the working cells to carry out their chemical reactions. Sweating during exercise depletes your body's water supply, which may lead to dehydration. Do not depend on your thirst to tell you to drink water. Try to drink at least 8 ounces of cool water for every 30 minutes of vigorous exercise. Use that water bottle!

42. Should additional salt be taken after exercise? There's plenty of salt from the food we eat and what we sprinkle on it. Excess salt can irritate the stomach, dry out body tissue, and raise blood pressure.

43. Will I get more out of my workout by speeding up the exercises? No. Smooth, controlled movements, properly executed through the full range of motion at an even tempo, are more important than speed.

44. Do all exercise programs give the same benefits? No, but everyone needs sustained, full-body, moderately paced aerobic activity.

45. What training effects happen to your body with aerobic exercise? (1) Your lungs will be able to process more oxygen. (2) The heart becomes a stronger muscle and pumps out more blood with each beat (stroke volume), which in turn allows you to increase oxygen delivery. (3) The blood vessels offer less resistance to blood flow, reducing the work of the heart. (4) The working muscles become more efficient at utilizing oxygen and nutrients for energy (ATP).

46. How long does it take to realize the benefits of a regular exercise program? It takes about four to 12 weeks for benefits to appear and up to six months for you to get "hooked" on exercise.

47. How many days of exercise can you miss before beginning to lose what you've gained? No more than three days in a row.

48. How long can you completely lay off exercise before you lose it all? From five to eight weeks.

49. What is muscle soreness and how do you get rid of it? Muscle soreness or delayed onset muscle soreness (DOMS) is soreness and swelling that becomes evident 8 to 10 hours after exercise and peaks between 24 and 48 hours. One hypothesis of soreness is the connective tissue theory, which suggests there is trauma and strain to the  connective tissues within muscle. Still, most recently, a newer theory explains that strenuous or unaccustomed exercise may cause the release of too many calcium ions from the sarcoplasmic reticulum. This ion accumulation may lead to micro damage of muscle proteins. Performing the same exercise (at a lesser intensity) that caused the muscle soreness will help to relieve it.

50. **What is that pain in the side sometimes felt in aerobics?** That sharp pain below the rib cage, often called a "stitch in the side," is usually caused by poor circulation in the muscles of the diaphragm or rib cage. Slow down your pace to allow the proper dilation of the affected blood capillaries, and the pain will go away.

51. **What is cross-training?** Cross-training is a method of integrating different fitness activities with the purpose of gaining or maintaining total-body fitness while reducing injuries. Each person must find the best mix of aerobics, resistance training, swimming, cycling, racquet sports, walking, and recreational sports. It is a very safe, effective, and balanced approach to fitness. Cross-training is extremely effective in a weight-loss program, as total work and hence caloric expenditure can be increased without increasing the risk of overuse injuries.

52. **Explain what steady state and lactate threshold mean?** Steady state in aerobic exercise represents a balance between the oxygen needs of the working muscles and their oxygen supply. As exercise intensity increases, the oxygen supply to the working muscles cannot meet all the oxygen needs of the muscles, and therefore, anaerobic energy systems will contribute more to the total energy production of the working muscles. The eventual transition of predominantly aerobic, oxidative energy production to include more anaerobic energy production during increasing exercise intensity is referred to as the lactate threshold, or onset of blood lactate.

53. **Why do you perspire more after you stop working out?** During exercise, your muscles need most of the blood to get oxygen for the activity. Upon the cessation of exercise, more blood is diverted to the skin to cool the body by means of sweat production. Also, during most modes of exercise, you are moving a lot, which helps sweat evaporate more efficiently during the activity.

54. **I only have time right before bed to exercise and am worried that it will impair my evening sleep patterns.** Interestingly enough, recent research has shown that vigorous exercise ending 30 minutes before bedtime failed to disrupt sleep.

55. **What causes muscle cramps?** New research on exercise-associated muscle cramping suggests the cramp occurs as a result of abnormal nerve activity from the spine, probably related to fatigue. Although not well understood, it is believed that tired muscles going through repeated shortening contractions are more vulnerable to cramping. Avoid overfatiguing workouts and incorporate regular stretching to best ward off muscle cramps.

56. **What does the term "MET" mean?** This term is used to describe energy expenditure of an activity. One MET is equivalent to the energy expenditure of a person at rest. It is expressed in terms of oxygen uptake (i.e., 3.5 ml O_2/kg/min). It is very much like a shorthand method of describing energy requirements. For instance, running 6 miles per hour is about 10 METs, whereas walking 3 miles per hour is about 3.3 METs.

57. **What are the limiting factors of flexibility?** With the muscles relaxed, and reflex mechanisms minimally involved, researchers have found the relative contributions of soft tissue to joint stiffness to be the following: joint capsule, including ligaments (47%), muscles and their fascial sheaths (41%), tendons (10%), and the skin (2%).

Nutrition

58. **Do foods with hydrogenated oils elevate cholesterol in the body?** Hydrogenated oils are known as trans fats, which do raise blood cholesterol. It is better to use tub margarine and avoid deep-fried foods such as fried chicken, french fries and doughnuts.

59. **How do you boost your HDL cholesterol?** HDL cholesterol is the 'healthy' cholesterol scavenger, that picks up excess cholesterol in your blood and takes it back to your liver where it's broken down and excreted. One major way to boost your HDL is to quit smoking if you smoke. Quitting smoking can increase your HDL cholesterol by up to 10 percent. Next, lose weight if overweight. Definitely get more aerobic exercise. Aerobic exercise for at least 30 minutes/day at a moderate intensity can increase HDL cholesterol by about 5 percent. Replace those saturated fats with healthier monounsaturated and polyunsaturated fats in your diet. Lastly, if you drink, moderation makes a difference. If you don't drink alcohol, don't start.

60. **Should I drink the smoothies that are so popular?** Several franchises now sell many types of "functional beverages," or smoothies. Most of these smoothies are made from fruit, juice, milk, yogurt, sorbet and special "boosts" of herbs, vitamins, fiber, protein and other substances. Some of the claims made by these stores are pretty outlandish, suggesting the drink can control stress, improve mood and increase energy. However, smoothies made from melons, carrots, berries and other produce truly do have healthy minerals, vitamins, fiber and phytochemicals. Perhaps the one downside of some of these smoothies is they "pack" a lot of calories; some have 500 to 700 calories per smoothie!

61. **Is it true that people who follow the Mediterranean lifestyle live longer?** Yes. Some studies show that persons who eat diets HIGH in fish, whole grains, fruit, nuts, vegetables and olive oil and LOW in meat, dairy products and saturated fats have healthier (and longer) lives. In addition, the Mediterranean lifestyle includes regular exercise (usually 30 minutes a day) with moderate alcohol intake and no smoking.

62. **Do vitamins enhance performance and give energy?** A **surplus** of vitamins probably won't improve your performance. Vitamins don't contain energy, food does, but vitamins **do** help metabolize food.

63. **What is the difference between saturated and unsaturated fats?** Saturated fats come predominantly from animals and are a suspected contributor to coronary heart disease. Unsaturated fats come from vegetables and are much healthier for you.

64. **What are the best foods to eat after aerobic exercise?** A selection of foods rich in complex carbohydrates (starches, not sugars), such as whole-grain breads and cereals, pastas, potatoes, leafy vegetables, green beans, broccoli, rice, peas, fruit, and grains.

65. **What is dietary fiber?** It is basically a type of complex carbohydrate made up of plant material that cannot be digested by the human body. Refining and processing foods removes almost all of the natural fiber. The main sources of dietary fiber are whole-grain cereals and breads, fruits, and vegetables. Optimal amounts of fiber in the diet increase gastric motility and therefore may reduce the incidence of diverticulitis, colon and rectum cancer, and obesity.

66. **Is it OK to drink beer after working out?** Alcohol is a diuretic, which means that it stimulates urine production. Following a workout you want to replenish your body with lost fluids. Consequently, drinking any alcoholic beverage before or after exercise is not recommended.

67. **Are natural vitamins better for you than manufactured vitamins?** No, your body can't distinguish the difference between vitamins manufactured in a laboratory and natural vitamins extracted from food.

68. **What's a good substitute for those high-fat potato chip snacks?**
Try pretzels. They are almost fat free. As a matter of fact, pretzels are one of the fastest-growing snack foods in the United States. However, there is good news for you chip lovers. There are now some new and improved chips that are low in sodium, fat, and calories. Read the labels at your supermarket. Look for the chips that are baked, not fried, and avoid chips made in hydrogenated oil. Remember to check the total fat content and serving size, too.

69. **Can you drink too much caffeine?** Most people have internal regulators that tell them when to stop drinking caffeine. However, 4 to 6 cups of coffee a day may result in symptoms referred to as caffeinism: breathlessness, headache, lightheadedness, and irregular heartbeat. Too much caffeine may also trigger a panic attack. For college students, caffeine-containing energy drinks have overtaken coffee as the primary source of caffeine. Most experts advise no more than 200 milligrams of caffeine consumption, which is about the same as two to three 5-ounce cups of coffee.

70. **Are there any foods that will make you more satisfied and less likely to binge?** Yes, some of the most filling foods include boiled potatoes, steamed fish, oatmeal, oranges, apples, whole-wheat pasta, grilled lean beef, baked beans, grapes, and whole-grain bread.

71. **What is grazing?** Grazing is an eating plan some people have adopted where they eat frequent little meals (up to six) spaced throughout the day. For some people, this may help to control the appetite, and they actually consume fewer calories. The one downside of this eating plan is the time it takes to plan, prepare, and then eat the smaller meals.

72. **What is this creatine supplement craze?** Creatine is an amino found predominantly in the muscles in the form of creatine phosphate, where it facilitates energy production. It also helps to reduce the lactic accumulation during intense exercise. Most investigations have shown that creatine supplements boost short-term muscle strength and power. However, it is important to note that the long-term effects of high doses of creatine are unknown.

73. **Is it true that when you eat out, you usually eat more calories than at home?** Yes. Large portion sizes and high-fat entrees burden most of this responsibility. Be aware that when you go out you are less likely to eat nutritious food. Forego eating appetizers, as they add to the calories. Perhaps split a dessert as opposed to ordering one for yourself. Also, most Americans neglect fruits and vegetables when eating out.

74. **What is the difference between brown rice and white rice?** The nutty flavor and chewy texture of brown rice is due to retention of the grain's bran. Brown rice has slightly more vitamin E, magnesium, and some other minerals. It also has more grams of fiber than white rice.

75. **I am so rushed to get things done that I am contemplating taking some of these liquid meal replacements on a regular basis.** Many of these liquid meals provide plenty of calories as well as a number of minerals and vitamins. But typically they do not provide the health promoting fiber and phytochemicals that are found in fruits and vegetables. So, this is not to discourage their consumption, but make sure you balance their intake with real meals.

76. **What does it mean when a food has the American Heart Association logo on it?** The red heart with white check mark means no more than 3 grams of fat, 20 milligrams of cholesterol, and 480 milligrams of sodium. The food must also have at least 10 percent of the daily value for one or more of these nutrients: protein, vitamin A, vitamin C, calcium, iron, or dietary fiber.

77. **What's the final scoop: Butter or Margarine?** Good question. Although margarine is indeed lower in saturated fat than butter, it's higher in trans fatty acids, which do contribute to high levels of cholesterol. Recent research does suggest that margarine is healthier. Also, it appears that soft tub margarine may be the best overall choice.

78. **What is the most common nutritional deficiency in the United States?** Iron deficiency. It affects some 8 million women of childbearing age and upwards of 700,000 toddlers.

79. **What is this new concept of training called periodization?** Although not really new, it is now being used regularly with recreational resistance-training enthusiasts. Periodization is most widely used in resistance training and involves systematically alternating high loads of training with decreased loading phases to improve components of muscular fitness. The system is typically divided into three cycles: (1) The microcycle, which lasts up to seven days; (2) The mesocycle, which can be from two weeks to a few months, is subdivided into preparation, competition, peaking, and transition phase; and (3) The macrocycle which is the overall yearly training period.

80. **What is carbo loading and how do you do it?** Carbo loading is a method of supersaturating your muscles with glycogen. It has been shown to improve endurance performance in events lasting over 90 minutes and is often used in competitive events. About seven days out from the event, begin by eating a diet high (60 to 70 percent) in high glycemic carbohydrates such as rice, pasta, and potatoes. Make sure you are getting adequate amounts of fat and protein as well. Drink plenty of water and increase your water intake four to eight cups (above normal) about two days before the event. Avoid dehydrating drinks and foods. As the event comes closer, remember to taper down your training so your body will be appropriately rested for the contest.

81. **What are phytochemicals?** They are not vitamins. They are not minerals. Phytochemicals are plant chemicals that offer great health benefits. They have been shown to protect against heart disease, cancer, diabetes, osteoporosis, and other medical conditions. The only way to get phytochemicals is to eat or drink them in fruits, vegetables, juices, nuts, and whole grain products.

82. **Can vegetarians get enough protein?** Yes. Vegetarians who eat a wide variety of foods each day will absorb a full complement of essential amino acids (the protein building blocks your body can't synthesize). Nuts, seeds, legumes, and many grains are good sources of protein. Also, vegetarians don't need to eat the complementary proteins at the same meal.

83. **Is it true that tea may possibly be a healthful beverage?** Yes, black and green teas (sorry, not herbal teas) appear to lessen cholesterol's damaging effect on your arteries, as well as protect against cancers of the skin and gastrointestinal tract. Make sure you steep tea for 3 minutes for the beneficial antioxidants in the leaves to enter the beverage.

84. **I like juice with pulp. Does it have more fiber than juice without pulp?** There is no significant difference in the fiber between juice with pulp and juice without it.

85. **What are trans fatty acids and are they good or bad for you?** Trans fatty acids are unsaturated fats that have had hydrogen added to them, making them more saturated. This chemical process helps to extend the shelf life of many foods, such as crackers, cakes, cookies, chips and unsaturated oils (such as corn and soybean). Regrettably, trans fatty acids raise your total cholesterol and LDL or "lousy" cholesterol. They can also lower your helpful or HDL cholesterol. In addition, trans fats, as they are sometimes called, are associated with increased risk of diabetes. When looking at food labels, the words *partially hydrogenated* indicate there are trans fats in the food, but the label typically doesn't say how much. Perhaps the best advice is to consume fewer processed and fast foods, as they have the most trans fatty acids.

Weight Management

86. **I read all the time that resistance training will really boost your metabolism. What does the research show on this?** Most resistance training programs show a 2 to 4.5 pound increase in muscle mass from 12 to 16 weeks of resistance training. The research also shows that with a 4.5 pound increase in muscle mass there is about a 50–100 calorie increase in metabolism. This is a lot lower than many product and program advertisements but still meaningful for weight management.

87. **My friend says that the best way to lose weight is just to do resistance exercise. Is this true?** Resistance training without diet does not show meaningful decreases in body weight. However, resistance training does show changes in body composition with the loss of body fat (2 to 4.5 lbs.) and the gain in muscle mass (2 to 4.5 lbs).

88. **Can you reduce the number of fat cells in your body?** No, only the size of the fat cells, not their numbers.

89. What is the fastest way to lose weight? Weight management is a balance of energy intake (food) and energy output (physical activity and exercise). The most efficient method for reducing "fat" weight is to do more aerobic exercise and resistance training and eat less food.

90. Can you lose weight by diet alone? Certainly, only you lose a lot of muscle tissue as well. You need exercise to preserve your muscle during reduced calorie living.

91. What is the recommended percentage of fat for men and women? From 5 to 15 percent for males 18 to 34 years of age, and from 16 to 28 percent for women 18 to 34 years old.

92. How is the percentage of body fat determined? Several popular methods include skinfold calipers, underwater weighing, and electrical impedance analysis.

93. Is there a difference between being overfat and overweight? Yes, overweight is only concerned with pounds. Overfat is concerned with the muscle/fat relationship. For instance, many professional football players are overweight by the familiar height/weight charts but have a low percentage of body fat (under 14 percent) and are certainly not overfat.

94. Do any of these fat burner supplements work? All of these fat-burning supplements contain some ingredients which manufacturers claim to either stimulate your metabolism or suppress your appetite. Most of these supplements have NOT gone through rigorous scientific investigations, because supplements are not regulated like foods. Alarmingly, there is no research on the long-term effects of these supplements or how they react with other supplements and medicines. For long lasting weight loss it is best to stay away from fat burner supplements and adopt lifestyle changes that promotes regular physical activity, lower calorie intake and healthy life behaviors.

95. What happens to your BMR as you age? Your BMR decreases with age primarily for two reasons. (1) There is often a loss of lean body tissue (muscle) with aging. (2) There is usually a decrease in activity while diet remains constant. This is all the more reason to keep exercising throughout your life!

96. In a typical group-exercise class consisting of 20 to 30 minutes of aerobic exercise, will loss of excess body fat be maximized at a lower or higher exercise intensity? Although it is true that exercising at a lower intensity burns predominantly fat and at a higher intensity predominantly carbohydrates, at the higher intensity, total caloric expenditure of fat and carbohydrates will be greater. If loss of excess body fat is the primary goal of the exercise program, a person should exercise at the highest intensity that can be safely maintained for the exercise bout.

97. Why does the mirror show your change of shape before the scale? Muscle is denser than fat. A pound of fat bulges out 18% more than a pound of muscle. Because you are adding muscle to your body as you shape up, you will often notice a loss of inches before a loss of weight.

98. Is yo-yo dieting risky for you? Let's face it, many well-intentioned diets do fail, which has concerned researchers that the losing and regaining of weight might be harmful to the body. However, new research with high blood pressure, which is a major risk factor for heart disease, shows that yo-yo dieting doesn't appear to have any physiological damage. However, in terms of emotional wellness, yo-yo dieting may lead to depression and low self-esteem.

99. Why don't diets work? Most diets, especially fad diets, are poorly designed plans that unrealistically restrict caloric intake. You lose weight initially, but these plans are not permanent weight-loss eating strategies, which people can incorporate into a regular lifestyle. Consequently, individuals usually return to their previous eating habits that encouraged the weight gain in the first place. Eating habits (and exercise) must be changed permanently for diets to be successful.

100. Will eating spicy foods help you burn more calories? Spicy foods, such as red or green chili peppers contain chemical compounds that can mildly boost your metabolism into high gear. Some studies suggest the effect only lasts about half an hour.

Disease

101. What is the difference in atherosclerosis and arteriosclerosis? Arteriosclerosis means hardening and thickening of the arteries. This occurs in most individuals as they age. Atherosclerosis is a type of arteriosclerosis. 'Athero' means paste, which refers to the buildup of plaque in arteries. Plaque, the clogging substance in arteries, is a mixture of cholesterol, fats, calcium, blood-clotting material and cellular debris.

102. What is angina pectoris? This is chest pain caused by too little oxygen reaching the heart. It often occurs during some type of physical exertion or elevated emotional excitement.

103. Please explain what is happening with a heart attack. A heart attack is referred to as a myocardial infarction. In this life-threatening situation, one of the arteries that supply blood to the heart muscle gets blocked. If a clot gets stuck in the artery, the lack of oxygen leads to heart tissue death.

104. Does heart disease affect women? Heart disease kills more women than any other disease, including cancer. A woman who has a heart attack is twice as likely as a man to die from it within the first few weeks.

105. Besides heart disease and diabetes, is obesity linked to any other diseases? Absolutely. It appears that obesity is associated with postmenopausal breast cancer, colorectal cancer, endometrial cancer, esophageal cancer, and kidney cancer. Obesity also increases the risk of stroke, hypertension, reflux disease, gallstones, and osteoarthritis. Remember, if overweight, a 5 to 10 percent decrease in starting weight can significantly improve many of these diseases.

106. **Who is affected most by osteoporosis and how can I prevent it?** Women are most affected, but it does occur in men, too. Presently, 10 million Americans have osteoporosis. Another 34 million citizens have osteopenia—this is a bone density that is below normal. To prevent this from occurring, do at least 30 minutes of "bone loading" exercise daily. Examples of this are walking, jogging and elliptical cross training. People between 19 and 50 years of age need to get at least 1,000 mg of calcium a day (1,200 for those individuals over 50 years). Try to also get at least 400 international units of Vitamin D daily. Lastly, eat plenty of fruits and vegetables, which are wonderful sources of potassium.

107. **What is the difference between Type 1 and Type 2 diabetes?** With Type 1 diabetes, the body's immune system destroys its own insulin-producing cells. Without insulin, blood sugar can't enter the cells where it is used for energy. In Type 2 diabetes, the cells become resistant to insulin. So, insulin shows up to the cell, but the cell is not working properly to allow insulin to do its job. When a fat or muscle cell becomes resistant to insulin, the sugar won't be driven into the cell and your blood glucose levels rise abnormally. Other consequences of this insulin resistance are high blood pressure, high blood fats and inflammation to the blood vessels.

108. **How do age and gender affect coronary heart disease risk?** Generally, the older you are, the greater your risk for heart attack. Between the ages of 35 and 44, coronary heart disease is less frequent in women than men, probably due to the production of the female hormone estrogen. Heart attacks appear to even out with older age.

109. **What are the four most important coronary heart disease risk factors?** Cigarette smoking, high blood pressure, abnormal levels of cholesterol, and physical inactivity.

110. **Is there any evidence that exercise can reduce heart disease?** Yes, a scientific study of over 16,000 Harvard alumni suggests that people who expend 2,000 calories per week in brisk exercise reduce death rates from heart disease by 25 to 33 percent, compared to those who do not exercise. Death rates decreased with increased weekly calorie expenditure (up to 3,500 calories) after which there was no advantage to those who did more exercise.

111. **What are free radicals and antioxidants?** Free radicals, also called reactive oxygen species, are unstable molecules produced by chemical reactions utilizing oxygen in the body's cells. A variety of external factors can promote free radical formation including smoking, drinking alcohol, and pollution. Antioxidants (vitamin C, E, and beta carotene—a precursor to vitamin A) protect the cells from free radicals by neutralizing the process of molecular oxidation that leads to their formation.

112. **What are the leading causes of death in the United States?** According to the National Center for Health Statistics, they are heart disease, cancers, strokes, injuries, chronic lung diseases, pneumonia, diabetes, suicide, AIDS, and homicide.

113. **What is cholesterol?** Cholesterol is a fatlike substance used to help build cell membranes, make some hormones, synthesize vitamin D, and form bile secretions that aid in digestion. Because fat can't mix with water, which is the main ingredient of blood, cholesterol's most important job is to help carry fat through your blood vessels. Before cholesterol can enter the bloodstream it is coated with a protein, referred to as a lipoprotein. Lipoproteins are transport vehicles in the circulation plasma that are composed of various lipids such as cholesterol, phospholipids, triglycerides, and proteins known as apoproteins. The major classes of lipoproteins are chylomicrons, very low-density lipoprotein cholesterol, low-density lipoprotein cholesterol, and high-density lipoprotein cholesterol.

114. **Which is the "bad" and "good" cholesterol?** The low-density lipoprotein cholesterol (LDL-C) is the primary transport carrier of cholesterol in the circulation. It is referred to as the "bad" cholesterol because too much cholesterol, from eating foods high in saturated fat, often leads to LDL-C pieces adhering to the inner walls of the blood vessels, narrowing the blood passages. On the other hand, the high-density lipoprotein (or helpful) cholesterol's (HDL-C) primary function is to transport cholesterol from the tissues and blood to the liver for excretion or recycling. It is referred to as the good cholesterol.

115. **What are triglycerides?** Triglycerides (TG) are fats that circulate in the bloodstream that provide energy for the body. It is uncertain whether high TG levels are associated with coronary heart disease. However, high TG levels are associated with diabetes, kidney diseases, and obesity. Steps to lower TG levels include cutting down on saturated fat, losing weight, exercise, and quitting smoking.

116. **I've heard recent reports that eating an egg or more a day isn't that bad for your heart after all.** More controlled research is needed. The American Heart Association and U.S. Department of Agriculture suggest no more than 300 milligrams a day of cholesterol intake. One egg has 215 milligrams of cholesterol, which leaves you only 85 milligrams for any other foods.

117. **Is it unhealthy to skip breakfast?** Some people think skipping breakfast will help you lose weight. That's incorret. Not eating breakfast actually may lead to weight gain, as your body goes into a starvation mode to retain stored fuel sources. Eating a light breakfast is more associated with successful weight loss and improved nutrition intake.

118. **What dietary substances are needed to prevent osteoporosis besides calcium and vitamin D?** Two other substances of importance are magnesium and potassium, which are both found in fruits, vegetables, milk and whole grains.

119. **I read a recent study that said high-fiber diets don't cut colon cancer.** Even if the study was well-conducted research, it is still only one study. Decades of research suggest that high-fiber foods are a protection against colon cancer. Remember, stay away from those sugary sweets that are consistently associated with colorectal cancer.

120. **How can I, as a young man, protect against prostate cancer?** Very wise preventative measure. Prostate cancer is the second leading cause of cancer in American men. Research confirms that diets high in fat, calories, and animal products are strongly associated with this deadly disease. Diets high in grains, cereals, soybeans, nuts, and fish, on the other hand, appear to have protective effects.

121. **What are the most common types of arthritis?** There are actually more than 100 different forms. Osteoarthritis is a wearing and tearing form that affects the fingers and weight-bearing joints (knees, back, hips). Rheumatoid arthritis causes irritating joint stiffness and swelling. Fibromyalgia leads to pain at different points of the body as well as insomnia, morning stiffness, and constant fatigue. Gout is caused when uric acid accumulates in the joints, specifically the big toe, knees, and wrists. Lupus can damage the kidneys, heart, skin, lungs, and joints.

122. **What does "prediabetes" mean?** The American Diabetics Association and the U.S. Department of Health and Human Services now use the term prediabetes to describe blood sugar levels that are higher than normal. Left untreated, many individuals will develop diabetes within 10 years. Losing 5 to 10 percent of body weight and doing at least 30 minutes of aerobic exercise daily will return blood sugar to normal.

123. **Is it true that eating big meals is associated with heart attacks?** Yes, a meal high in calories may quadruple the risk of a heart attack in those at risk to coronary heart disease. Researchers theorize that the large meals may temporarily elevate blood pressure, which could break loose some atherosclerotic plaque in an artery. This free-floating plaque in the bloodstream could lead to a blood clot in a coronary artery. Enjoy your meals, but eating in moderation is good for heart health as well as weight control.

124. **I thought all I had to be concerned with for heart disease is checking my cholesterol and triglyceride levels. What's this new protein associated with heart disease?** There's a new clue in understanding heart disease. It involves how the body's immune system works. The development of atherosclerotic plaque (hardening of the arteries) triggers the body to begin an inflammatory process to try to heal the artery wall. With some people, this inflammation process leads to ruptures of the atherosclerotic plaque. This could break off a piece of plaque into the bloodstream and be a precursor to heart attacks (if the clot goes to the heart) or a stroke (if the clot goes to the brain). The best blood predictor for this inflammation process, which is very easy and inexpensive to measure, is called hs-CRP for high sensitivity C-reactive protein.

    If you have high levels of hs-CRP you can reduce the risk of heart disease by eating a diet low in saturated fat and cholesterol, lose weight if you are overweight, do regular aerobic exercise, stop smoking if you smoke, and control your blood pressure.

125. **What is heartburn?** Heartburn occurs when gastric fluids, which are very acidic to better digest food in the stomach, enter the esophagus. If this happens frequently, the esophagus may develop scar tissue and be more susceptible to developing cancer.

Sixteen Exercise Myths

1. **If you are thin, you're fit.** Sorry, but being thin is no indication of how efficient your heart, lungs, and muscles are. Body composition testing has demonstrated that many thin people actually have more than the recommended percentage of body fat. You've got to exercise!

2. **Sit-ups get rid of stomach fat.** Wouldn't that be nice! This myth is based on spot reducing. Research clearly shows that exercises for specific body areas firm the muscles, but fat reduction comes from aerobic exercise and a decrease in caloric intake. Fat is reduced proportionally throughout the body.

3. **Weight lifting develops aerobic capacity.** Lifting weights does elevate the heart rate, but this type of exercise does not improve aerobic capacity. It does develop firmer and shapelier bodies.

4. **Sweat loss means weight loss.** You do lose weight temporarily when you sweat, but this is mostly water loss, not fat loss, and is regained as you quench your thirst. Similarly, "sauna sweat suits" induce a temporary water loss and can be dangerous if you get too dehydrated.

5. **Aerobic exercise and jogging cause a woman's breasts to sag.** There is no evidence documenting this claim. However, a good supportive bra is recommended for comfort.

6. **Extra protein makes you stronger.** Eating extra protein will not directly add muscle bulk. It is true that protein functions to build and repair muscles. However, the key to building muscle is to strength train. Some people try to gain muscle just by consuming more protein—that's not enough to stimulate muscle growth by itself. The extra protein will be used for energy or more likely converted to and stored as fat.

7. **A candy bar (sugar) before exercise will give you fast energy.** Actually, candy bars, honey, and other sweets quickly enter the bloodstream and stimulate a tremendous release of insulin. The extra insulin during exercise causes your blood sugar to drop, leading to faster exhaustion.

8. **Go for the burn.** Listen to your body. Any type of pain is a warning signal. None of the physiological mechanisms associated with "the burn" have been demonstrated to have beneficial results for you.

9. **Lifting weights gives women bulky muscles.** Women do not produce enough male hormones to allow for large muscle growth. And women don't have as much muscle fiber or mass as a man. Lifting weights will help a woman develop a better figure.

10. A low resting heart rate means you're fit. Exercise can lower your resting heart rate. However, this alone does not indicate a person's fitness level.

11. Electrical stimulation can reduce fat, increase tone, and build strength. Wow, all those results for just sitting there with electrodes attached to you. How appealing! Though electrical stimulation devices are used by physical therapists for rehabilitation purposes, they are quite ineffective as an effortless exercise alternative.

12. Muscles turn to fat when you stop exercising. There are many retired athletes who seem to prove this. However, fat cannot change to muscle (or vice versa). When you stop exercising, your muscles start to waste away and lose their firmness. If you continue to eat a substantial diet (as many of these athletes do), the overconsumption of food will result in larger fat cells.

13. Cellulite is a unique type of fat. Cellulite is excess fat bulging between connective tissues under the skin giving that "orange peel" appearance. Rubbing creams don't work. Lessen the appearance of cellulite through aerobic conditioning, body firming exercises, and a proper diet.

14. **There is major physiological deterioration as we age.** Although there is a slight tendency toward reduced performance with age, in general, people continuing their aerobic exercise maintain much of their aerobic efficiency and exercise capacity.

15. **Free weights are better than machines.** Not so fast. There are advantages of both modes of resistance training.

   ▶ **Machines:** Machines ensure that you go through a standardized movement pattern, while targeting specific muscles. The newer exercise devices also have built-in safety features for the user. Several machine designs provide an effective variable resistance through the movement range to make exercises more challenging. Lastly, the exerciser doesn't have to balance the weight when training with machines.

   ▶ **Free Weights:** For many trainers, having to balance the weight, as is the case with free weights, is an advantage because this involves more stabilizing muscles. Free weights offer much more versatility in their use from the way you hold the weight, as well as your position using the weight. The inexpensive cost of free weights is a major advantage. Finally, free weights allow the user to go through different planes of motion than machines, which have fairly fixed planes of motion (although some companies have now developed this feature with some machines).

16. **Weight gain is inevitable as you get older.** Actually, this is more related to a reduction in physical activity as opposed to age. With inactivity a person loses muscle mass, which reduces the metabolic rate at which they expend calories. At the same time, this inactivity leads to a gradual accumulation of body fat. The best way to prevent this is to include aerobic exercise and resistance training into your daily life.

Fitness Trivia Quiz

Try this trivia quiz to learn some additional fitness facts!

1. True or False: The average foot walks more than a thousand miles a year.

2. Is it training **affect** or training **effect**?

3. True or False: Muscles waste away if they are not used.

4. What percent of your body weight is water? 40%, 60%, 80%.

5. True or False: There are over 600 muscles in the human body.

6. What unique dynamic ability do muscles possess?

7. Which is the single most important source of fuel for your body? Fats, carbohydrates, proteins.

8. What is the junction of two bones called?

9. What is the term for enlargement of muscles?

10. True or False: It only takes 23 seconds for blood to circulate through your entire body.

11. One pound of fat equals how many calories?

12. The average heart beats how many times a minute? 62, 72, 82.

13. Name four of the six classifications of nutrients you need to eat.

14. True or False: Vitamins contain calories.

15. True or False: Vitamins are named as alphabet letters because, when they were discovered, scientists did not know their chemical structure and could not give them "proper" names.

16. Lack of what mineral is associated with "tired blood"?

17. True or False: Your appetite increases in cold weather.

18. Fast-twitch muscle fiber, known for its explosive characteristics, is referred to as _____ muscle fiber. (red or white)

19. What is the longest muscle in the body?

20. What is the largest tendon in your body?

21. Your skeleton comprises what percent of your body weight? 15%, 25%, 35%.

22. How many years does it take for the cell structure of your skeleton to completely rejuvenate itself? 5 years, 7 years, 10 years.

23. True or False: Two-thirds of exercise-induced injuries are caused by overuse.

24. Which is the only joint in the body with 360 degrees of rotation?

25. True or False: Sweat is your body's way of cooling off.

26.   What is the single most preventable cause of death?

27.   True or False: Women live approximately eight years longer than men.

28.   True or False: Current estimates in the United States indicate that over 65 percent of all adults have a weight problem.

29.   How many glasses of water should you drink each day?

30.   True or False: Drinking cool water during exercise is beneficial because it reduces internal body heat.

Answers on page 178.

Health Trivia Quiz

Try this trivia quiz to learn some additional health facts.

1. What is the least favorite day of the workweek?

2. A specific fear associated with a place, thing or person is called a _____ .

3. True or False: In the United States more women smoke than men.

4. True or False: Studies show that 85% of teenagers who occasionally smoke two to three cigarettes (a day) go on to become nicotine dependent.

5. Women can reduce infant mortality by _____ % if they stopped smoking. 10%, 20%, 30%.

6. True or False: Drinking alcohol helps a person attain restful sleep.

7. True or False: Alcohol increases one's creativity.

8. If someone is addicted to alcohol, what is the best way to change this addiction?

9. True or False: Pathological gamblers are not intelligent people.

10. True or False: Shopaholics often make unnecessary purchases because the process of buying is often more important that what is bought.

11. True or False: Workaholics are driven perfectionists who would rather work than play.

12. True or False: If you consume a lot of protein you also need to increase your water intake.

13. True or False: Eating foods with fiber helps you manage your weight better.

14. True or False: If you eat too much sugar you will get diabetes.

15. Which is more nutritious: fruit juices or fruit drinks?

16. What constitutes a low-in-sodium food?

17. What is a processed food?

18. What neurotransmitter in the brain is associated with well-being and depression?

19. What cycle determines your body's blood pressure, temperature, hormone output, cell division, and sleep/wake cycles?

20. Is it better to try to go to bed at the same time nightly or wake up at the same time every morning?

21. What is the leading cause of nonfatal injuries in the United State and second-leading cause of death from injury?

22. What age group is prone to getting bored?

23. The causes of 90 percent of high blood pressure are uncertain and referred to as _____ .

24. Heart attacks occur most frequently on what day?

25. The heart's built-in heartbeat comes from where?

26. Is heart disease reversible?

27. What type of tumor contains tissues not typically found where they originate?

28. What is it called when unwanted cells in the body spread like seeds to other parts of the body?

29. What is a fake solution or fake cure to a health problem called?

30. What is the single most important thing you can do to prevent the transmission of infectious organisms?

Answers on page 179.

Answers to Fitness Trivia Quiz

1. True
2. Training effect
3. True
4. 60%
5. True
6. They contract
7. Carbohydrates
8. A joint
9. Hypertrophy
10. True
11. 3500 calories
12. 72
13. Carbohydrates, fats, proteins, water, vitamins, minerals
14. False—vitamins do not contain calories
15. True
16. Iron
17. True
18. White
19. Sartorius on the thigh
20. Achilles tendon
21. 15%
22. 10 years
23. True
24. Shoulder
25. True
26. Cigarette smoking
27. True—One of the primary reasons for this is the higher incidence of heart attack deaths among men before the age of 55.
28. True
29. 8 to 10 eight-ounce glasses
30. True

How Did You Do?

26 or more correct	You are Exceptional!!!
21 to 25 correct	You can be Proud!!!
16 to 20 correct	You should Try Harder!!!
15 or less correct	You are Not Alone!!!

Answers to Health Trivia Quiz

1. Monday
2. Phobia
3. False—Actually, more men (31%) smoke than women (26%). However, women who do smoke are heavier smokers and usually start at younger ages.
4. True
5. 10%
6. False—Alcohol interferes with normal sleep rhythms.
7. Although drinking alcohol may reduce one's inhibitions, it does nothing to improve your productivity or creativity.
8. The majority of alcoholism practitioners agree that giving up drinking entirely is the best solution.
9. False—They often have superior intelligence.
10. True
11. True—Workaholics are obsessed with their career and making a living.
12. True—Protein requires seven times more water than carbohydrate and fat for metabolism.
13. True—Foods high in fiber are low in fat and have a bulking effect in your stomach that aids in the feeling of fullness.
14. False—Diabetes results from two problems: an increased insensitivity of the body's cells in the presence of insulin and an insufficient production of insulin by the pancreas.

15. Fruit juice, which will be low in sodium and high in potassium.
16. 140 mg of sodium or less per serving.
17. Food that has been cooked, mixed with additives, or altered in texture.
18. Serotonin
19. Your circadian rhythm
20. Most experts recommend trying to get up at the same time of morning.
21. Falls
22. Late teens and early 20s. Boredom is the opposite of anxiety. Anxiety arises when one has low levels of skills and high levels of challenge.
23. Primary (or essential) hypertension.
24. Mondays between 8 a.m. and 9 a.m.
25. The pacemaker known as the sinoatrial node.
26. Yes, through stress-relieving techniques, a heart-healthy diet, and exercise.
27. Malignant tumor
28. Metastasize
29. Quackery
30. Wash your hands often.

How Did You Do?

26 or more correct   You are Exceptional!!!
21 to 25 correct   You can be Proud!!!
16 to 20 correct   You should Try Harder!!!
15 or less correct   You are Not Alone!!!

GLOSSARY

A

adenosine triphosphate (ATP) The high-energy substance found in cells from which the body gets its energy.

aerobic exercise Physical activities such as brisk walking, running, cycling, swimming, rowing, and aerobic dancing that rely heavily on oxygen for energy production.

aerobic metabolism Processes in which energy (ATP) is supplied when oxygen is utilized while a person is working.

agonist The muscle identified as the prime mover of an action.

anaerobic exercise Short-term output of energy for muscular contraction supplied by the phosphagen and glycolytic energy systems.

android obesity Male pattern of fat deposition in the abdominal region. Associated with cardiovascular disease and other diseases.

antagonist A muscle that causes movement at a joint in a direction opposite to that of its agonist.

arteriosclerosis An arterial disease characterized by the hardening and thickening of vessel walls.

atherosclerosis A form of arteriosclerosis in which fatty substances deposit in the inner walls of the arteries.

B

ballistic Fast, bouncy movement.

basal metabolic rate The energy required to sustain life while in a fasted and rested state.

blood pressure The force that blood exerts against the walls of the blood vessels and that makes the blood flow through the circulatory system.

blood sugar The concentrations of sugar (called glucose) in the blood.

body composition The relative amounts of muscle, bone, water, and fat in the body. Body composition is usually divided into fat and fat-free mass.

C

calorie A unit of measure for the rate of heat or energy production in the body.

carbohydrates Foodstuffs primarily used for vigorous muscular activity. Found in the body as glucose and glycogen.

cardiac output The amount of blood pumped by the heart in one minute. It is the product of heart rate and stroke volume.

cardiorespiratory endurance The capacity of your heart, blood vessels, and lungs to function optimally during sustained vigorous exercise.

cardiovascular disease A group of diseases of the heart and circulatory system.

cartilage The resilient covering of the weight-bearing surface of bones. The cartilage absorbs shock and prevents direct wear on the bones.

cellulite A label given to lumpy deposits of fat commonly appearing on the back of the legs and buttocks of some individuals.

cholesterol A fatlike substance that plays an important role as a building block for cells and hormones. It is obtained from eating foods of animal origin and also produced by the body. Elevated levels are associated with increased risk of heart disease.

circuit training Exercises performed in sequence from station to station. Usually done at a rapid pace.

contraindication A sign or symptom suggesting that a certain activity should be avoided.

cool-down An "aerobic cool-down" refers to a gradual decrease of vigorous aerobic conditioning. A "workout cool-down" refers to the stretching and relaxation phase at the end of a training session.

coronary heart disease The impairment of the coronary arteries of the heart associated with a buildup of cholesterol and fatty substances on the inner artery wall.

creatine phospate Molecule that rapidly helps to resynthesize ATP.

cross-training Selection and participation in more than one physical activity on a consistent basis.

D

dehydration The condition that results from excessive loss of water.

depression Prolonged emotional sadness that persists beyond a reasonable length of time. Often occurs with symptoms such as insomnia, headaches, exhaustion, irritability, loss of interest, impaired concentration, and feelings that life is not worth living.

diabetes mellitus A metabolic disorder in which the body is unable to regulate the level of glucose in the blood.

E

energy The capacity or ability to perform work.

exercise heart rate The heart rate during aerobic exercise that will result in cardiorespiratory benefits. Also referred to as "training heart rate."

F

fat A food substance used as an energy source. It is stored when excess fat, carbohydrate, or protein is ingested.

fiber The indigestible polysaccharides found in the leaves and stems of plants.

flexibility The range of motion of a joint or group of joints.

frequency Refers to the number of workouts needed per week to establish a training effect.

G

glucose Energy source (in the form of sugar) transported in the blood.

glycogen The form in which glucose is stored in the body (primarily in the muscles and liver).

glycolysis The metabolic breakdown of glucose.

gynoid obesity Female pattern of fat deposition in the thighs and gluteal areas that does not carry the same risk as upper body obesity.

H

heart attack Death of a part of the heart muscle caused by a lack of blood flow.

heart rate The number of times the heart beats per minute.

homeostasis The tendency of the body to maintain internal equilibrium and regulation of bodily processes.

hyperglycemia An elevation of blood sugar.

hypoglycemia Low blood sugar.

hypertension High blood pressure.

hypertrophy An increase of mass in a muscle from resistive exercise.

I

insoluble fiber Cellulose, lignin, and hemicellulose that add bulk to the contents of the intestine, accelerating the passage of food remnants through the digestive tract. Insoluble fiber may help to reduce colon cancer of the digestive tract.

intensity The level of physiological stress on the body during exercise.

isokinetic contraction A contraction in which the tension is constant throughout the range of motion.

isometric (static) contraction A contraction in which tension is developed but there is no change in the length of the muscle.

isotonic contraction A dynamic contraction in which the muscles generate force against a constant resistance.

L

lactate Lactate is the product of a side reaction in glycolysis.

lactate threshold The point during exercise when blood lactate begins to increase considerably. It is a good indicator of the highest sustainable work rate.

lordosis An abnormal curvature of the low back.

M

maximum heart rate The highest your heart will beat during aerobic exercise.

maximum oxygen consumption The maximal rate at which the muscles can consume oxygen in one minute.

metabolism The sum total of all physical and chemical processes occurring in the body.

mitochondria Organelles within the cells that utilize oxygen to produce ATP.

mitochondrial respiration metabolic reactions that take place in the mitochondria of cells to produce ATP for energy.

minerals Inorganic substances of the body including sodium, potassium, chloride, calcium, phosphorous, magnesium, sulfur, and at least 14 trace minerals that perform several necessary roles in the body.

monosaccharide Simple sugars such as table sugar and honey.

muscular endurance The ability to exert force (not necessarily maximal) over an extended period of time.

N

nutrients The basic substances of the body obtained by eating foods.

O

obesity An above-average amount of fat in the body. In males 25 percent or greater and in females 32 percent or greater is considered obese.

overload To exercise a muscle or group of muscles with resistance greater than normally encountered.

overtraining A condition from too much exercise characterized by a lack of energy, a decrease in performance, and bodily aches and pains.

osteoporosis The thinning and weakening of the bones that is seen predominantly in postmenopausal women.

overweight Excess weight for one's height regardless of body composition.

P

perceived exertion A subjective rating of the intensity of a particular exercise activity.

polysaccharide The joining of three or more simple sugars to form a starch.

protein A food substance that sustains basic structural properties of the cells and serves as a source for hormones and enzymes in the body.

R

recovery heart rate The gradually declining heart rate following the cessation of aerobic exercise.

repetition A repetition represents each time an exercise movement is completed.

resting heart rate The average heart rate prior to initiating any physical activity.

S

saturated fat Animal fat and fat found in dairy products and eggs that contribute to atherosclerosis.

set Group(s) of repetitions. One set might consist of 10 repetitions.

skinfold A pinch of skin and subcutaneous fat from which total body fat may be estimated.

spot reducing A myth that fat can be specifically reduced from one body area through exercise.

static stretch A stretch that is held.

strength The capacity of a muscle to exert near maximal force against a resistance.

stress It is a nonspecific response of the body to pleasurable and painful demands made on it.

stretch reflex A reflexive contraction of a muscle that is being stretched.

stroke volume The amount of blood pumped by the left ventricle of the heart per beat.

T

testosterone A sex hormone appearing in much higher concentrations in males than females.

triglyceride A compound consisting of three molecules of fatty acid and glycerol. It is the main type of lipid found in the body.

U

unsaturated fat The molecules of a fat that have one or more double bonds and are thus capable of absorbing more hydrogen. These fats are usually of vegetable origin.

V

valsalva maneuver Condition occurring when a person lifts heavy weights while holding the breath. The glottis closes and intrathoracic pressure increases, hindering blood flow to the heart.

vitamins Nutrients required in microamounts that are essential to numerous bodily functions.

W

warm-up The first portion of a workout, designed to prepare the body for the vigorous exercise to follow.

THE MUSCLE SYSTEM

Muscle and Exercise Chart

This chart lists the major muscle groups and specific exercises presented in this book, as well as the opposing groups.

Deltoids
Push-up Variations
Dips
Side Lateral Raises
Chest Press
Shoulder Press

Pectorals
Chest Press
Wide-arm Push-ups
Flys

Trapezius
Power Rows

Latissimus Dorsi
Standing Rows

Biceps
Bicep Curls

Triceps
Tricep Extensions
Dips
Pike Push-ups
Chest Press

Abdominals
Crunch Variations

Obliques
Twisting Crunches
All-Around Crunches
Rope Pull Crunches

Erector Spinae
Back Extensions
Horizontal Side Bridge
Rolling Side Bridge
Bird-Dog Exercise

Gluteus Maximus
Squats
Lunges
Prone Leg Lifts
Power Exercises
Back Thigh Lifts

Rectus Femoris, Vastus Lateralis, Vastus Medialis
Squats
Lunge Variations

Biceps Femoris, Semitendinosus, Semimembranosus
Squats
Lunge Variations

Gracilis, Adductor Longus
Inner Thigh Variations
Hip Adduction
Wide Squats

Tensor Fasciae Latee, Gluteus Medius
Hip Abduction

Gastrocnemius and Soleus
Heel Raises

Examples of Opposing Muscle Groups

Biceps vs. Triceps
Deltoids vs. Latissimus Dorsi
Pectorals vs. Rhomboids and Trapezius
Quadriceps vs. Hamstrings
Abdominals vs. Spinal Extensors
Thigh Abductors vs. Thigh Adductors

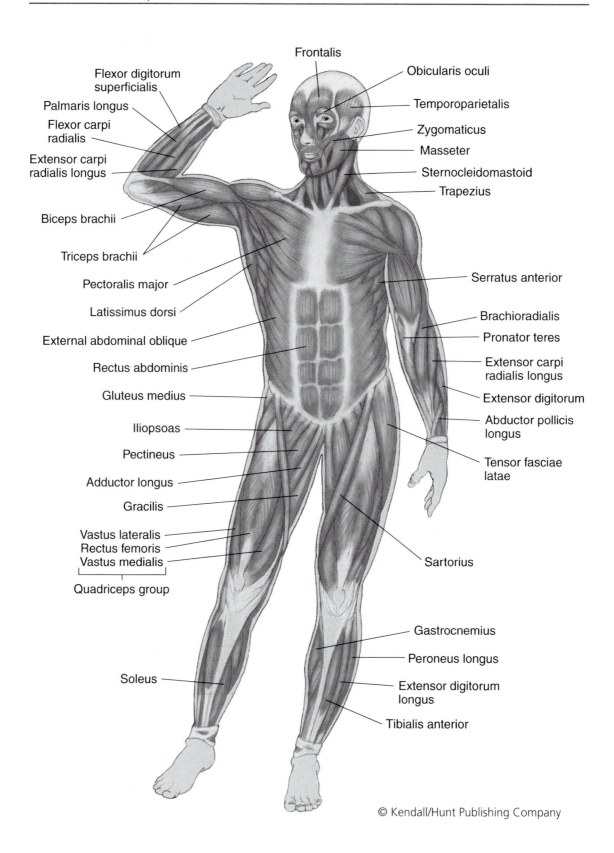

Frontalis

Flexor digitorum superficialis

Palmaris longus

Flexor carpi radialis

Extensor carpi radialis longus

Biceps brachii

Triceps brachii

Pectoralis major

Latissimus dorsi

External abdominal oblique

Rectus abdominis

Gluteus medius

Iliopsoas

Pectineus

Adductor longus

Gracilis

Vastus lateralis
Rectus femoris
Vastus medialis

Quadriceps group

Soleus

Obicularis oculi

Temporoparietalis

Zygomaticus

Masseter

Sternocleidomastoid

Trapezius

Serratus anterior

Brachioradialis

Pronator teres

Extensor carpi radialis longus

Extensor digitorum

Abductor pollicis longus

Tensor fasciae latae

Sartorius

Gastrocnemius

Peroneus longus

Extensor digitorum longus

Tibialis anterior

© Kendall/Hunt Publishing Company

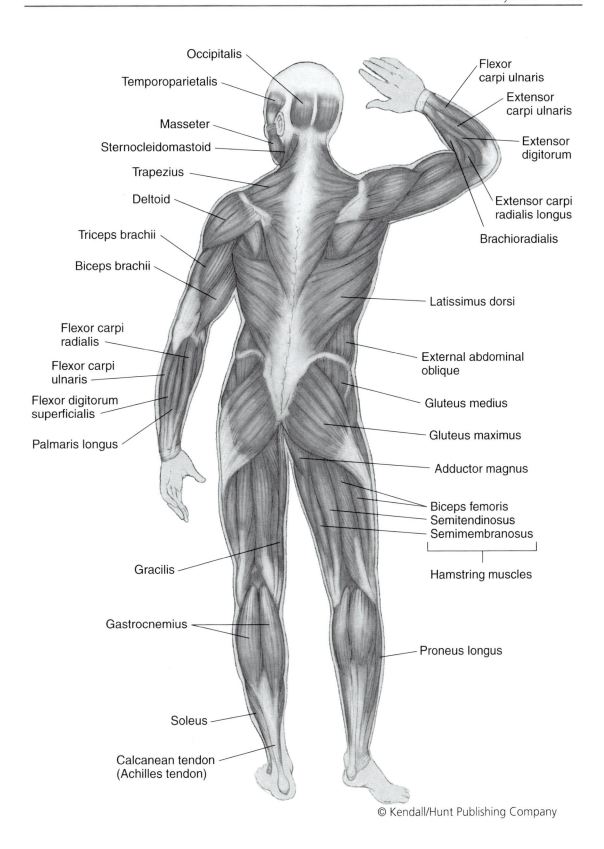

Occipitalis

Temporoparietalis

Masseter

Sternocleidomastoid

Trapezius

Deltoid

Triceps brachii

Biceps brachii

Flexor carpi radialis

Flexor carpi ulnaris

Flexor digitorum superficialis

Palmaris longus

Gracilis

Gastrocnemius

Soleus

Calcanean tendon (Achilles tendon)

Flexor carpi ulnaris

Extensor carpi ulnaris

Extensor digitorum

Extensor carpi radialis longus

Brachioradialis

Latissimus dorsi

External abdominal oblique

Gluteus medius

Gluteus maximus

Adductor magnus

Biceps femoris
Semitendinosus
Semimembranosus

Hamstring muscles

Proneus longus

ACSM Publishes Updated Position Stand on the Quantity and Quality of Exercise

The new American College of Sports Medicine quantity and quality Position Stand paper is an update that cites over 400 publications from scientific reviews, epidemiological studies, clinical studies, meta-analyses, consensus statements and evidence-based guidelines. The purpose of this ACSM Position Stand paper is to present evidence-based direction to health and fitness enthusiasts and professionals for the development of individualized exercise training programs for apparently healthy adults of all ages.

CARDIORESPIRATORY FITNESS RECOMMENDATIONS	
Variable	**Evidence-Based Recommendation**
Frequency	≥5 day/wk moderate* intensity or ≥3 days/wk vigorous** or a combination of both on ≥3–5 days/wk
Intensity	Moderate and/or vigorous is recommended for apparently healthy adults
Time	30–60 minutes at a moderate intensity or 20–60 minutes at a vigorous intensity or a combination of both
Type	Purposeful, continuous, rhythmic exercise involving the major muscle groups of the body
Pattern	Exercise may be performed in one continuous session per day or in multiple sessions of ≥10 min to accumulate the desired duration
Progression	Progress intensity, duration and frequency gradually until desired goal is attained

*Moderate intensity includes exercise that is fairly light to somewhat hard, or a rating of perceived exertion (RPE) of 12–13.
**Vigorous exercise includes exercise that is somewhat hard to very hard, or a RPE of 14–17.

NEUROMOTOR EXERCISE RECOMMENDATIONS	
Variable	**Evidence-Based Recommendation**
Frequency	≥2–3 days/week
Intensity	Not determined at this time
Time	≥20–30 min/day may be needed
Type	Exercises that improve balance, agility, coordination and gait, particularly for older adults to improve/maintain physical function and to prevent falls
Volume	The optimal volume of repetitions and sets is currently unknown

RESISTANCE EXERCISE RECOMMENDATIONS	
Variable	**Evidence-Based Recommendation**
Frequency	Major muscle groups should be trained 2–3 days/week with a 48-hour rest between sessions for muscle groups
Intensity (Strength)	40–50% of 1RM or very light to light load for beginning older persons and for beginning sedentary persons 60–70% of 1RM or moderate to hard load for novice to intermediate adult exercisers ≥80% of 1RM or hard to very hard load for experienced weight lifters
Intensity (Endurance)	<50% of 1RM or light to moderate load
Intensity (Power)	20–50% of 1RM or very (very) light to light load in older adults
Repetitions	10–15 repetitions to improve strength in beginning, middle aged and older persons 8–12 repetitions to improve strength and power in most adults 15–20 repetitions to improve muscular endurance in most adults
Sets	Single set training for novice and older adults 2–4 sets are recommended for strength and power of most adults ≤2 sets for muscular endurance
Rest	2–3 minutes of rest between multiple set training

FLEXIBILITY EXERCISE RECOMMENDATIONS	
Variable	**Evidence-Based Recommendation**
Frequency	≥2–3 days/week of stretching the major muscles groups; greater gains will be attained if done daily
Intensity	Stretch to the point of slight discomfort or feeling of tightness in muscle
Time	30–60 seconds of static stretching holds for older persons 10–30 seconds of static stretching holds for most adults
PNF Stretches	3–6 seconds of a muscle contraction at 20–75% of maximum intensity followed by 10–30 seconds of an assisted stretch
Pattern	2–4 repetitions of each stretch is advocated
Volume	Provide a total of 60 seconds of stretching time per target muscle group for any stretching method utilized

Adapted from: Garber, C.E., Blissmer, B., Deschenes, M.R., Franklin, B.A, et al. (2011). Quantity and quality of exercise for developing and maintaining cardiorespiratory, musculoskeletal, and neuromotor fitness in apparently healthy adults: Guidance for prescribing exercise. *Medicine & Science in Sports & Exercise,* 43 (7), 1334–1349.

New ACSM Position Stand: Physical Activity, Weight Loss and Weight Regain

Presently 66.3% of U.S. citizens are either overweight and/or obese. Weight loss in overweight/obese persons of as little as 3% to 5% of body weight (although 10% reduction is encouraged) has shown improvements in high-density lipoproteins (the good cholesterol), glucose utilization (for the prevention of diabetes), and reduction in blood fats and other risk factors of cardiovascular disease.

In the new ACSM position stand, the authors define weight maintenance as a <3% change in body weight, where as a 5% or greater change in body weight is considered a clinically significant change. The term "clinical" infers involving a medical observation, treatment, practice or diagnosis.

How Much Physical Activity Is Needed for Clinically Significant Weight Loss?

It is recognized that most studies showing clinically significant weight loss (≥5% of body weight) demonstrate this with energy restriction (i.e., eating fewer calories) combined with physical activity to create a larger negative energy balance (i.e., more calories expended than consumed). Physical activity in the form of aerobic exercise between 225 and 420 minutes/week results in the greatest weight loss. For best practices, the ACSM position stand recommends accumulating 250 to 300 minutes of aerobic exercise each week. You can accumulate this aerobic exercise in ≥10-minute exercise bouts throughout each day. Also ACSM notes that regular resistance training (2–3 times a week) is a must for the maintenance and/or increase of muscle mass, as well as for an increase in daily energy metabolism (called resting metabolic rate).

What About Weight Regain After Weight Loss?

It appears that many individuals are capable of losing weight with the long-standing challenge being how to maintain this reduced body weight. Consistent physical activity is the best predictor of sustained weight management after weight loss. And, when it comes to preventing weight gain, 'more is better'. The report specifies that individuals who have lost >10% of their body weight in 24 months, and did not gain it back, are participating in 275 minutes of aerobic exercise a week.

Adapted From: Donnelly, J.E., Blair, S.N., Jakicic, J.M., Manore, M.M., Rankin, J.W., & Smith, B.K. (2009). Appropriate physical activity intervention strategies for weight loss and prevention of weight regain for adults, 41(2), 459–469.

Do You Know Your Important Risk Factor 'Numbers'?

All exercise enthusiasts need to be aware of their clinical 'numbers' for well being. This section serves as an informative resource for identifying the many 'numbers' involved in clinical and health parameters that are not covered in other sections of the text.

Cholesterol, Triglycerides and C-Reactive Protein

Cholesterol, which is vital to the body, is used to assemble cell membranes, produce sex hormones, and form bile acids, which are required for the digestion of fats. When certain blood cholesterol levels are elevated, some of the excess is deposited in the arterial walls, thus the risk for heart disease is increased (See Table 1 for levels). Elevated blood triglycerides (fats) are also an independent risk factor for coronary heart disease, meaning that some particles of fat can collect on arterial walls and lead to atherosclerotic plaque.

Current research additionally suggests that inflammation plays a role in the formation of atherosclerosis. C-reactive protein (CRP), a substance the body produces in response to inflammation and infection serves as a very good marker for heart disease risk. The blood vessel test for inflammation is called the high-sensitivity CRP or hs-CRP.

TABLE 1: CHOLESTEROL, TRIGLYCERIDE AND hs-CRP LEVELS	
Total Cholesterol	
Desirable	Less than <200 mg/dL
Borderline high	200–239 mg/dL
High	>240 mg/dL
LDL ("Bad") Cholesterol	
Optimal	<100 mg/dL
Near optimal	100–129 mg/dL
Borderline high	130–159 mg/dL
High	160–189 mg/dL
Very high	>190 mg/dL
HDL ("Good") Cholesterol	
Low	<40 mg/dL
High	≥60 mg/dL
Triglycerides (Fats in the Blood)	
Normal	<150 mg/dL
Borderline-high	150–199 mg/dL
High	200–499 mg/dL
Very high	≥500 mg/dL
C-Reactive Protein (hs-CRP)	
Low CVD risk	<1.0 mg/dL
Average CVD risk	1.0–3.0 mg/dL
High CVD risk	>3.0 mg/dL

Data from American Medical Association, 2001 and American Heart Association, 2010

Body Mass Index

Body mass index (BMI) is an alternative screening tool to percent fat measurement that can be used to categorize individuals as underweight, overweight, or obese, and to observe changes in body weight that may be associated with health problems (See Table 2).

Example Calculations:

With the metric system, the formula for BMI is weight in kilograms divided by height in meters squared.

Weight = 120 kg, Height = 193 cm (1.93 m)

Calculation: $120 \div (1.93)^2 = 32.2$

The BMI formula for weight in lbs and height in inches is weight (lb) divided by height $(in)^2 \times 703$

Weight = 150 lbs, Height = 65 inches

$(150 \div \{65\}^2) \times 703 = 24.96$

TABLE 2. INTERNATIONAL CLASSIFICATION OF BMI RANGES FOR ADULTS	
BMI Value	**Classification**
<16.00	Severe thinness
16–16.99	Moderate thinness
17–18.49	Mild thinness
18.5–24.99	Normal Range
25.0–29.9	Overweight (Pre-Obese)
	Obesity
30.0–34.9	Class I
35.0–39.9	Class II
≥40	Class III
Adapted from World Health Organization, 2010	

Waist Circumference

Measuring waist circumference helps screen for possible health risks that come with overweight and obesity. If most of your fat is around your waist rather than at your hips, you're at a higher risk for heart disease and type 2 diabetes. This risk goes up with a waist size that is greater than 35 inches for women or greater than 40 inches for men. To correctly measure your waist, stand and place a tape measure around your middle, just above your hip bones. Measure your waist just after you breathe out.

DISEASE RISK ACCORDING TO WAIST CIRCUMFERENCE		
Men	**Women**	**Disease Risk**
<35.5	<32.5	Low
35.5–40.0	32.5–35.0	Moderate
>40.0	>35.0	High

Other Laboratory Tests

Exercise enthusiasts often receive their medical reports from their primary physician. Table 3 describes selected blood variables usually tested.

TABLE 3. OTHER SELECTED BLOOD VARIABLES OF CLINICAL IMPORTANCE		
Selected Blood Variable	**Normal Value**	**Description of Variable**
Hematocrit	40-52% (men) 36-48% (women)	The percent volume of red blood cells in whole blood.
Hemoglobin	13.5–17.5 g/dL (men) 11.5–15.5 g/dL (women)	Protein molecule within red blood cells that carries oxygen and gives blood its red color
Potassium	3.5–5.5 meq/dL	Electrolyte and a mineral. It helps keep the water (the amount of fluid inside and outside the body's cells) and electrolyte balance of the body. Potassium is also important in how nerves and muscles work.
Blood Urea Nitrogen	4–24 mg/dL	Measure of the amount of nitrogen in the blood in the form of urea, and a measurement of renal function.
Creatinine	0.3–1.4 mg/dL	Reliable indicator of kidney function. Also a waste product of muscles from exercise.
Iron	40–190µ/dL (men) 35–180 µ/dL (women)	Mineral needed for production of hemoglobin, the main protein in red blood cells that carries oxygen.
Calcium	8.5–10.5mg/dL	Builds and repairs bones and teeth, helps nerves work, assists in muscle contraction, helps blood clot, and facilitates heart function.
Data from Heyward, V.H. (2006). Advanced Fitness Assessment and Exercise Prescription, (5th edition), *Human Kinetics*		

Be Proactive with Your 'Numbers'

The exercise enthusiast now has these clinical values at his/her fingertips to promote actions steps for wellbeing improvement. Take a proactive approach as you strive for optimal health.

Caloric Expenditure Chart

You can easily estimate the number of calories you expend during aerobic exercise activities. To determine the number of calories expended, multiply the total number of minutes of activity times the calories per minute. For example, a 110-pound woman doing 20 minutes of continuous aerobic dance would expend approximately 172 Calories ($8.6 \times 20 = 172$).

CALORIC EXPENDITURE CHART FOR SELECTED AEROBIC ACTIVITIES	
(Aerobic dance, cycling, brisk walking, rope skipping, rowing on a machine, running, skating, and swimming.)	
Your weight in pounds	**Calories Expended per minute**
95–104	8
105–114	8.6
115–124	9.0
125–134	9.7
135–144	10.3
145–154	11
155–164	11.5
165–174	12
175–184	12.7
185–194	13.3
195–204	13.7
205–214	14.2
215–224	14.7
225–234	15.2
235–244	15.7
245–254	16.2
255–264	16.7
265–274	17.2
275–284	17.7
Values may vary from individual to individual.	

Total number of minutes of aerobic exercise   _____

Calories expended per minute according to your weight   _____

Your estimated caloric expenditure   _____

Estimating Your Caloric Needs

You can estimate the breakdown of your daily intake of carbohydrates, proteins and fats. Follow the steps below.

To estimate your daily caloric needs, first multiply your weight by 16 (if you are moderately active) or 12 (if you are relatively sedentary).

1 gram of carbohydrate	= 4 calories
1 gram of protein	= 4 calories
1 gram of fat	= 9 calories

Daily nutritional needs

Carbohydrates	= 58% of your daily calories
Proteins	= 12% of your daily calories
Fats	= 30% of your daily calories

Weight (lbs): _____ × 16 or 12 = _____ (Estimate of daily caloric needs)

Carbohydrates

Carbohydrate Calories per Day

Estimate of calories per day: _____ × 0.58 (58%) = _____ calories/day

Carbohydrate Grams per Day

Divide the above product by 4: _____ ÷ 4 = _____ grams/day

Proteins

Protein Calories per Day

Estimate of calories per day: _____ × 0.12 (12%) = _____ calories/day

Protein Grams per Day

Divide the above product by 4: _____ ÷ 4 = _____ grams/day

Fats

Fat Calories per Day

Estimate of calories per day: _____ × 0.30 (30%) = _____ calories/day

Fat Grams per Day

Divide the above product by 9: _____ ÷ 9 = _____ grams/day

INDEX